PROMOTION: DENIED

PROMOTION: DENIED

The harrowing true story of racism, cover-up, betrayal and vigilante justice at the United States Air Force Academy

By Lt. Col. Joseph W. Hoffler, USAF-Ret.

Hertford Free Press

For further information, please contact:
Jhoffler@comcast.net

Book design by
Arbor Books, Inc.
19 Spear Road, Suite 301
Ramsey, NJ 07446
www.arborbooks.com

Printed in the United States of America

Promotion: Denied: The harrowing true story of racism, cover-up, betrayal and vigilante justice at the United States Air Force Academy
Lt. Col. Joseph W. Hoffler, USAF-Ret.
1. Title   2. Author   3. Non-fiction

Library of Congress Control Number: 2007924641

ISBN 10: 0-9794686-0-4
ISBN 13: 978-0-9794686-0-5

In Tribute to
Ruby Kimbrough Hoffler

April 17, 1940–May 31, 2006

In memory of my beloved wife, Ruby Kimbrough Hoffler,
who passed away on May 31, 2006, at the age of sixty-six.
After serving four years in the Air Force, Ruby married
2nd Lt. Joseph W. Hoffler on December 10, 1965,
and began her nineteen years as a military wife.
During those nineteen years, Ruby served as a
volunteer in many Air Force organizations.
A loving wife, and a devoted mother and grandmother,
she stood by my side for more than forty years.
She is greatly missed and this book is dedicated to her.

TABLE OF CONTENTS

AUTHOR'S NOTE

The incidents of racism in the Air Force recorded in this book are, regrettably, true. They were the work of a few individuals who were allowed to misuse authority and pervert justice to enforce their prejudices. Their names have been changed so the story can be told without focusing on specific people.

I wish to express profound appreciation to my operations officer and first sergeant, who risked their Air Force careers in their fight against racial discrimination. They were truly the "freedom riders" of the 1980s.

Even today, the disease of racism has not been cured. The young men and women of color who are at the beginning of their careers in the Air Force should at least be forewarned.

That is my hope in writing this book.

PROLOGUE

"The only thing necessary for the triumph of evil is for good men to do nothing."

—Edmund Burke

Once a generation, a hero comes along whose arrival on the scene changes everything. The American Civil Rights Movement is star-studded with heroes, ordinary people who, when faced with extraordinary circumstances, stood up and said, "No more. This injustice stops with me." We need look no further for stellar examples. There was Marian Anderson, banned from performing at Carnegie Hall for being black, triumphantly singing at the Lincoln Memorial on Easter Sunday, 1939. It's hard to forget the brave second baseman Jackie Robinson of the Brooklyn Dodgers breaking Major League Baseball's color barrier in 1947, then the humble seamstress Rosa Parks refusing to give up her bus seat in Montgomery, Alabama, in 1955. Remember, too, James Meredith, desiring nothing more than an education, daring to attend the University of Mississippi in 1962 even at the expense of death threats and a police escort.

The American military is also full of examples of heroic African-Americans who battled racial discrimination and won, going on to build successful military careers. Think about the great Generals B.O.

Davis, Chappie James, and, in more recent times, Colin Powell, the son of immigrants and a Vietnam veteran, who later became the chairman of the Joint Chiefs of Staff.

Now the time has come to add the name of Joseph W. Hoffler to the ranks of American civil rights heroes who battled the U.S. military. An ordinary man faced with extraordinary circumstances, Joseph W. Hoffler had the courage to sacrifice a promising military career to stand tall and fight injustice. He sacrificed his privacy and that of his family to stand up to the United States Air Force Academy. Now he is coming forward to expose the deeply ingrained institutional racism that denied him a well-deserved promotion to colonel and ultimately forced him out of the military after a highly decorated twenty-two year career.

I first met Joseph W. Hoffler, or, as I affectionately call him, "Colonel H.," when I joined his squadron, the 7625th Security Police Squadron, at the United States Air Force Academy in Colorado Springs, Colorado, in the fall of 1983. I served as Lt. Col. Hoffler's operations officer and he immediately impressed me as a strong leader: fair, even-tempered, with a quick mind and a generous heart. As the operations officer, I had first-hand knowledge of the unethical and illegal actions by academy officials and their efforts to cover up their activities.

Even after our squadron was shaken by the assignment of a new chief of staff, Lt. Col. Hoffler reacted calmly, with dignity and self-respect. He refused to believe that the United States Air Force he had loved so much and had served so valiantly would allow one colonel to use his personal biases to destroy the careers of accomplished and dedicated black members of the Air Force. I stood by Lt. Col. Hoffler during that difficult time and was always impressed by the way he handled himself, never stooping to the level of those vicious USAF Academy senior officers who were working against him but always believing that the truth, and justice, would prevail in the end.

It has taken more than twenty years but, as Lt. Col. Hoffler says, "There is no statute of limitations on righting racial wrongs." Finally, in the pages of this book, the whole story can at last be told. The following pages reveal a sordid tale of corruption by senior Air Force Academy officials and the hijacking of the very system that should have protected minorities from racism.

My hope is that this book, with its tough, uncompromising tale of prejudice, abuse and retribution, will serve as a wake-up call to the American taxpayers. Is the United States Air Force Academy, with its sexual assault scandal and its high-tech "lynching" of Lt. Col. Hoffler, the kind of organization that the average American wants his or her tax dollars supporting? While the superintendent of the USAF Academy, the director of security police, and various other Air Force agencies stood by and did nothing to stop them, a group of rogue senior officers at the United States Air Force Academy dispensed their own brand of vigilante justice against Lt. Col. Hoffler, the first African-American squadron commander in the academy's history. If such a serious miscarriage of justice can happen to Lt. Col. Hoffler, what are the implications for younger, less-decorated minority members of our military? When rampant racism and prejudice are allowed to run unchecked, don't we all pay the price in the long run?

Bravo to Lt. Col. Hoffler for having the courage to take on the Air Force Academy single-handedly and for challenging our military, our government, and our leaders truly to be the best that they can be.

Operations Officer
7625th Security Police Squadron
USAF Academy, CO
1983-1985

CHAPTER 1

WHY I DECIDED
TO TELL MY STORY

July 2004

"AFA seeks help in recruiting minorities." The headline of *The Gazette*, my local newspaper, stopped me cold. I read it again, pausing to consider each word. "AFA seeks help in recruiting minorities: Inner-city congressmen not helping, school says." A chill ran down my spine. "Not again," I whispered. "I won't allow another miscarriage of justice against minorities at the Air Force Academy."

It was not yet 7 a.m. on a Saturday morning, July 24, 2004, and I was enjoying my morning coffee at my home in Colorado Springs, looking out my window at the Rocky Mountains and a beautiful view of Pike's Peak. I was sixty-four years old, a retired Air Force lieutenant colonel, happily married and enjoying a prosperous second career as a business owner, mentor and educator.

Even with all my successes, seeing this headline took me right back to the early 1980s, when, as an black officer, I saw my career destroyed by institutional racism and a group of racist superior officers who conspired to deny me a promotion to colonel thereby ending my military career.

1

To provide a bit of background, I, along with other black officers, had been recruited by the Air Force Academy in 1979 and 1980. Among the other black officers recruited were a colonel, who was assigned as the commander of the Civil Engineering Squadron, and two female captains, who were assigned to the personnel branch.

I had had a stellar career until then, when a racist chief of staff and inspector general, along with a handful of underlings, set out to ruin me and other black personnel. Apparently some whites thought that the command element in the Security Police Squadron at the academy was "too black." After these incidents came to light, the United States Air Force Academy wouldn't help me, particularly the superintendent who, unlike his two predecessors, was very insensitive to the plight of black Air Force personnel. The Air Force itself refused to help, along with the military establishment and even the Department of Defense and members of Congress. They all failed to ensure fair and equal treatment for all members of the Armed Forces, regardless of race. And now the academy was pushing to recruit minority cadets?

I sipped my coffee and returned to the article.

At a time when the Air Force Academy is trying to boost minority enrollment, the officer-training school says it isn't getting enough help from congressmen representing inner cities. The academy gets seventy-five percent of its students through the congressional appointments, but representatives in high-minority, inner-city districts often offer few prospective cadets or none at all, academy Superintendent Lt. Gen. John Rosa said.

Oh, no. I feared for these young men and women whom I pictured recruited by the academy and then left unsupported by the hierarchy once they arrived. "I've got to do something," I said to myself. "These young people are being recruited like I was, only to be exploited in order to meet a quota, and then abandoned to racists who can end their careers."

I put down the newspaper and called to Ruby, my devoted wife of thirty-eight years. "Look, dear." I pointed to the article. "The academy is recruiting minority cadets." Ruby sighed. "Joseph, just let it go," she warned. "Think about your health." I had had triple bypass open-heart surgery in 1998 and I knew that Ruby worried about the stress. We had been through so much and she wanted me to enjoy my golden years in peace. "You've been fighting this thing for two decades," she reminded me. "You've gone through all the military channels with no result. Three congressmen haven't helped."

"I know," I said. "But maybe things have changed. Ever since the sexual assault scandal at the academy, the Air Force has been more willing to address faults within its own system. If they can admit a failure to properly investigate cases of sexual harassment, they might also admit their history of racism and finally make some changes."

"This may be another waste of time," Ruby countered. "You'll get all worked up again for nothing. The NAACP did not help you; the Rainbow Coalition did not help you. You're on your own."

Her brown eyes twinkled. "And don't tell me you're thinking about bringing down that old box again," she said.

I kept a battered old Xerox box on the top shelf of my bedroom closet. It was full of old papers about the congressional investigation, files and reports documenting what had happened to me and my numerous and futile attempts to find justice. When I thought about everything that had been done to me, I was furious. I had to file a Freedom of Information Act request just to get this information from the headquarters of the Air Force inspector general.

The box contained irrefutable documentation, including a letter from the inspector general of the Air Force Academy illegally denying me a copy of an investigation conducted on me and my squadron. The box also included documentation of the recruitment and rewarding of false witnesses against me, along with the intimidation of, and retaliation against, those who attempted to tell the truth.

The box held proof of the cover-up of illegal activities by senior Air Force Academy staff, including tampering with Air Force personnel records. Every once in a while I would go through that old box, wondering if justice would ever be done. Before I could answer Ruby's question, our thirty-six-year-old daughter, Patricia, who was living with us at the time, joined us for breakfast. She had my eighteen-month-old grandbaby and namesake, Joseph, in her arms.

"Patti, Dad's on it again," Ruby said ruefully. "The paper said something about minority recruitment at the academy."

"Oh, no!" Patti replied. "Not the box again!" Patti handed Ruby the baby, took my hand and looked me straight in the eye. "Dad, don't get all worked up," she pleaded. "You promised to be around for Joseph's college graduation. Your health is more important than the case. The Air Force treated you unfairly but there's nothing you can do now."

I touched Patti's cheek. I appreciated her and Ruby's concern and certainly didn't relish the prospect of another David vs. Goliath battle. Before going any further I made a phone call.

My former operations officer had always supported me. Although our friendship had lasted more than twenty-three years, our origins could not have been more different. I was a black man raised in the South by a proud, successful family with historic ties, while he, an Italian-American, came from the rough streets of New York City. He had put his own military career on the line for me and I had never forgotten his sacrifice. He resigned his Air Force commission following my case and joined the federal government. In fact, he had been only four blocks from Ground Zero on September 11, 2001, and had received a commendation for his brave actions that day.

"Captain, you are not going to believe what was in today's paper," I said to him, now living in upstate New York. After I summarized the article, I heard surprise in his voice.

"I can't believe it," he said. "Look what happened to you, Colonel H."

"I know, but I've got to do something," I insisted.

"But what? You've tried everything."

I revealed what had been formulating in my mind all morning. "There's one thing left. I can put the word out, tell my whole story, and let the American taxpayers decide if this is the kind of military they want their tax dollars supporting."

"Talk to journalists?" he asked. "You've already approached several reporters."

"You're right. That's why I'm going to write a book," I replied. "I'm going to get the whole story down on paper for everyone to see."

As we talked, the enthusiasm grew. Though he was concerned about my health, he ultimately agreed with me. "Let's go for it," he said. "I'm pumped, Colonel H. I'm really pumped. It's worth one more try."

Buoyed by his support, I made a few more calls. I talked to my 32-year-old son, Brian, in Denver and he took the middle line: concerned for my health but supportive. "If you're really serious, go for it," Brian advised. "If this is going to bring you closure," he paused, "and if this means you can finally take that box down off the shelf forever, then go for it, Dad."

My final phone call was to my longtime friend. Her late husband had also been a lieutenant colonel stationed at the Air Force Academy. She and her husband were at the academy before I was, so her knowledge of the systematic mistreatment of black officers went deep. "Sarah, have you read this morning's *Gazette*?" I asked.

"Not yet," she replied. When I read her the headline, she sighed. "They're doing it again. Recruiting blacks, even though nothing has been done to improve the situation up there." Because the Air Force Academy was situated on a hill, it was sometimes referred to as "up there." "The academy has made great strides in improving the treatment of female cadets, but nothing has been done to help cadets who are racial minorities," Sarah continued. "But Joseph, what can you do now? The Air Force will never admit what they did to you."

"Sarah, I can't let the new recruits have their careers ruined by racist senior officers."

After speaking with Sarah, I understood the enormous task I was taking on, and at a time in my life when I should be relaxing, reaping the rewards of years of hard work. Ruby and Patti rolled their eyes as I brought out the dreaded Xerox box. It was full of glowing officer efficiency reports detailing my outstanding record as a military officer, beginning with my enlistment as a twenty-two-year-old college graduate in 1962. I rose to the rank of lieutenant colonel in the Air Force security police and the Minuteman Missile Launch Officer fields. Later I commanded the 513th Security Police Squadron at the RAF (Royal Air Force) base in Mildenhall, England.

During my tenure, the 513th Security Police Squadron received the first "excellent" rating during an ORI (operational readiness inspection) for a Security Police Squadron in the more than fifty-year history of the USAFE (United States Air Force Europe). It was also named the "Best Security Police Squadron" in the Air Force for 1978. Following those distinguished achievements, I was recruited by the academy in 1978 to serve as a role model to young minority cadets. There was never a single negative mark against me until 1984, when, ten days after being named my supervisor, the USAF Academy chief of staff made it his personal vendetta to deprive me of a well-deserved promotion and end my career, simply because I am black.

For the past twenty years no one has listened. I leafed through the papers in my box. Maybe there's a different culture and attitude "up there." Following the sexual assault scandal in 2003, the academy superintendent retired.

Changes were implemented and a number of female officers assigned to the Air Force Academy were promoted. However, it had been nearly nineteen years since the academy's first and only permanent African-American professor retired. Maybe the sexual harassment scandal has opened the door, I reasoned. They've got the attention of the secretary of the Air Force and the Air Force chief of staff. I tried to convince myself that maybe now is the time. My senator from Colorado wouldn't help, but now he has helped female cadets who were sexually harassed.

The last time I had written to the Air Force calling attention to the problem of racial discrimination at the academy, they had responded,

"We appreciate your letter but you retired in 1984 and it's been too long." My reply at that time was, "I didn't know that there was a statute of limitations on racism."

Looking through my battered Xerox box, my mind was made up. In an effort to prevent these same career-ending actions against other minority officers or senior NCOs, I decided to write this book. "The story must be told," I said, as I closed the box. No other young black military service member should suffer as I did.

Later that day while playing with Joseph, I overheard my wife and daughter talking. "Dad isn't going to let this die, is he?" Patti asked.

"I'm afraid not," Ruby answered. "Your father took what happened very hard. He wasn't naïve enough to think that there weren't bigots in the Air Force. But that Air Force agencies and senior commanders would stand idly by and refuse to help? That was too tough to take."

Patti nodded. "Poor Dad."

"Your father loved the Air Force," Ruby continued. "He was so proud to be an officer. Obtaining an Air Force commission in 1964 did not come easily to an African-American. Not only that, your dad relished his role as a mentor to African-American cadets and a role model for African-American junior officers and enlisted personnel."

I saw Ruby smile from across the room. "You know, Patti, Dad used to sponsor cadets. It seemed like every weekend we had cadets over for a barbecue or just to relax."

Patti laughed. "Mom, I remember you telling the black female cadets where to get their hair done! And Dad talking about how proud he was to be an Air Force officer and how they should continue to carry the banner of responsibility. I remember Dad taking cadets to the airport when they went on leave and picking them up again when they returned. We always had cadets around the house!" Both women became silent, lost in thought. "Mom," Patti asked slowly, "what really happened between Dad and the Air Force?"

"I don't know," Ruby acknowledged. "He won't talk about it. The only person who really knows is the captain. He fought alongside him and, over the years, I have heard him and the captain talk, but your father has never told me the whole story."

"Never?"

"That's right. And it's very strange because over the nineteen-plus years we spent in the Air Force, your dad and I talked about everything else. I guess this hurts too much. Your dad loved the Air Force and gave it his all."

"Mom, I want to know what really happened."

"So do I, Patti. That's why Dad's going to write this book. So the whole world will know."

Turning away from Ruby and Patti, I looked down at baby Joseph in my arms. "For you, too," I whispered. "I'm writing the book so you will know the truth about what racists at the U.S. Air Force Academy did to your granddad."

CHAPTER 2

THE INVESTIGATION STARTS

By 1984 I had a twenty-one-year record of distinguished military service and since 1979, I had been assigned to the U.S. Air Force Academy in Colorado Springs. At the academy I was "two-hatted," meaning that I was both the director of security police and the commander of the 7625th Security Police Squadron. I had received "outstanding" ratings on all of my OPRs (officer performance reports), completed all of my professional military education (PME) and earned an MBA. I was looking forward to a promotion to colonel. I had no idea how dramatically my life was about to change.

On March 19, I received a telephone call from a lieutenant colonel who was a group commander in the cadet wing, which meant he commanded ten cadet squadrons. I thought, *He's trouble.* I was aware of a previous serious lapse in judgment on his part. He had been the officer in charge of cadet basic training, which was held on the Air Force Academy grounds in an area called Jack's Valley, located in a wooded area less than a mile northwest of the academy's north gate. He had approved a training program that called for the cadets to wear battle dress uniforms and carry fake rifles at night while pretending to "attack" the security policeman posted at the north gate. The security policeman nearly fired on the cadets, but he was well trained in the rules of firearm engagement and withheld his fire. Fortunately, no one was hurt.

I couldn't believe that an officer had approved such a dangerous maneuver. When I met with him afterwards, he acknowledged that his actions were "dumb." Personally, I thought his actions were much worse than that. *Now he wants to talk?* I wondered. What could that be about?

"Joe," Lt. Col. Jones said over the phone, sounding casual, "I'm looking into some things for the new chief of staff. Could you meet me at my office at fourteen-hundred hours?" Never did he mention that he was investigating a complaint for the inspector general. I told him okay and hung up. His call, although unexpected, did not concern me. I certainly had no reason to believe that I was under investigation.

Ten days earlier Deputy Chief of Staff Smith had taken over as chief of staff, so I assumed that perhaps he wanted to learn how he could assist his commanders and provide better support. (During this era, the chief of staff at the Air Force Academy operated as a base commander.) When I entered the cadet group commander's office later that day, Lt. Col. Jones again told me that he was "looking into some things for the new chief of staff."

I had no idea at that point that he was in fact conducting an inspector general (IG) investigation on me, even though he was required, by Air Force regulations, to alert me to that fact. He also didn't mention that I was a suspect in a case of theft of government property, even though, by regulation, he was required to alert me to that fact as well. As a suspect, I should have been informed of my Article 32 rights under the Uniform Code of Military Justice (UMCJ), but I wasn't. Among documents in the Xerox box was a ruling from the academy's legal office that would confirm that all of these legal errors had been made during the investigation, but at that point, on that sunny afternoon in March, I had no idea what was going on.

"Joe, tell me about A1C Brett Stover's duties in the squadron," he said.

"At the moment, A1C Stover is considered 'non-effective' and not performing security police duties," I explained.

"Why?" he asked. "And what exactly do those duties consist of?"

"Well, the command element, the commander and first sergeant, received information that there were certain," I searched for the right words, "issues in his personal life that made us question whether A1C Stover should be issued a weapon."

"What issues are those?"

"Well, two ex-security policemen who are now deputy sheriffs in Teller County came to my office and told me that they heard that Stover was going to harm someone in the unit over a lieutenant's wife. The first sergeant also confirmed that Stover was being sued in Small Claims Court. It appears that he purchased a truck from a civilian in town and failed to pay him. He also left a note with his present supervisor that the troops called a 'suicide note.' I asked the base therapist to evaluate Stover. That evaluation will determine whether he is fit to return to duty."

"How many non-effectives do you presently have in your squadron?" the lieutenant colonel asked.

"Stover is the only one at present," I replied. "We have had maybe five or six total in my four and a half years at the academy."

"Is it the normal procedure for a security policeman to have a mental evaluation?"

I answered, "One of a security police commander's primary duties is to ensure that security policemen who are issued a weapon are mentally stable.

"When information is brought to our attention that may indicate an emotional problem, security police commanders are required by Air Force Regulation 125-126 to recommend that person for a mental evaluation. Stover's status is routine in a Security Police Squadron. It is not a disciplinary action, only precautionary to protect him and maybe someone else from possible harm. We aren't qualified to determine a person's mental state; only a licensed therapist can do that." I paused. "Some of Stover's fellow flight members are concerned," I added. "They asked that he be evaluated because they fear his actions."

"Sounds serious," he said.

I stepped closer to his desk. "Darn right it is serious. We're issuing a security policeman a weapon and ammunition," I explained. "As a commander I have to ensure that all of my troops are protected. In the civilian police force, a recruit has to be at least twenty years old. In the Air Force, we issue them weapons at eighteen years of age. Two or three years can mean a lot when it comes to maturity. This is quite different from two airmen in personnel arguing over a woman, and they are sitting across the desk from each other, armed with nothing more than ballpoint pens," I added for illustration. "In the Security Police Squadron, we are issuing weapons and ammunition." The investigating officer didn't react, so I continued. "The Air Force Academy, unlike most Air Force bases, is an open base." (This changed after September 11, 2001, by the way.) "Being an open base means that anyone, including criminals, can drive right onto the base.

"Several times in the past year, my troops have been asked to assist Colorado Springs police and El Paso County sheriff deputies with searches for civilian suspects on the academy grounds. Just like in the civilian police force, there has to be great trust in the people you work with; in a crisis, you have to trust that your backup is reliable.

"A few years ago, there was a homicide on the academy grounds. A civilian employee shot and killed his supervisor and escaped into the woods on the academy. And the security police had to pursue this armed suspect on the grounds until the civilian police arrived. Thanks to the great work of the security police, no one else was injured and the suspect was safely apprehended. If you are a policeman in trouble you need dependable backup. Right now that dependability among the troops does not exist regarding Stover.

"His actions, like leaving that note with his supervisor, have been deemed strange by his fellow security policemen, and as his commander I am very concerned."

I thought that, having explained the situation to him, our meeting would be over, but instead he began a series of bizarre and unsettling questions.

"Joe, have you ever gambled with the airmen?" he asked.

"NO," was my emphatic reply. My mind raced. "Three years ago, a day before Christmas break, I walked in on a friendly five-and-ten-cent poker game at an old house on the academy grounds that served as the squadron's training building. Frankly, I was checking to see that the punch was only punch and not spiked with anything. After tasting it, I was satisfied it was only punch.

"Everyone was in the holiday spirit, joking around, and one of the players asked me to watch his hand while he went to the bathroom," I explained, trying to remember the details of that long-ago incident. "I stood by the table, but I never touched the cards. When he returned, I told them to finish the hand and go home for the holidays. Then I left the building. I did not gamble."

The investigating officer's expression didn't change. "I see," he said evenly. "Joe, do you allow football pools in your squadron?"

By now I was suspicious of his questioning, but I maintained my composure. I had done nothing wrong, so I assumed I had nothing to worry about.

"My troops had been asking for years if they could have a football pool," I explained. "So I checked with the legal office first. A major in the legal office said there were football and World Series pools all over the academy. 'Just don't get involved and don't play,' he told me." After being pressured by the academy IG and the investigating officers, he changed his statement and denied telling me it was okay.

Unlike other Air Force bases, the Air Force Academy had a Division I football team, so people on the base lived and breathed college football. "So as a morale issue in the squadron, after receiving the okay from the legal department, I told the staff sergeant who was requesting me to allow a football pool that yes, it was okay to have one, as long as it was voluntary, limited to E-5s and below and didn't cost more than $1 to enter. It was strictly for morale. Since the security police had to work long hours at every home football game it gave the troops something to talk about during down times. I never took part," I told the inspector general's investigating officer.

He raised his eyebrows. "I see." Then without further words, he changed topics. "Now what about the piece of Plexiglas that the Security Police Squadron's supply NCOIC gave you?"

I was shocked. He was questioning me about a piece of Plexiglas? What was going on here, anyway? I took a deep breath. "About four or five months ago, I saw some small scrap pieces of Plexiglas out by the dumpster behind our building. I told the Security Police Squadron's supply NCOIC if he had any more scrap pieces, I could use them for a project. I wanted to make coasters out of them because during my staff meeting, attendees would place coffee cups on my table and leave cup rings. Sometime later the Security Police Squadron's supply NCOIC said, 'Colonel, I have some leftover Plexiglas. Do you want it?' I said yes and asked him to put it in my car. So he did. There was nothing to hide. This all took place in broad daylight."

The academy's investigating officer continued his icy stare.

"The Plexiglas had no monetary value," I explained. "It had been designated for the scrap pile."

"Uh-huh," he said. "And have you ever made bets with the younger airmen in your squadron?"

"No," I said. "Once a staff sergeant asked me if I had change for the soda machine and I gave it to him. Since I did not have change for the whole dollar, he gave me a dollar bill and I jokingly told him that I would keep the change to cover a bet he owed me. Later that day, I got change for a dollar and gave him his change."

My mind flashed back to his mention of A1C Brett Stover. Stover had been standing around when I shared that joke with the staff sergeant. A1C Stover must have taken the comment out of context. Of course Stover was not around when I gave the staff sergeant his change. "Why don't you question the staff sergeant about this incident?" I suggested. (I later learned that the USAF Academy inspector general's investigating officer never questioned the staff sergeant. As with everything else in this case, he simply took Stover's word; he did not want to hear anything contrary to Stover's version.)

"Have you ever used profanity towards A1C Stover?" he asked.

"Once," I acknowledged. "However, that was totally out of character. I don't use profanity in my daily life and I especially don't use it towards my troops." The pieces fell into place. Stover was key to this whole issue.

"This was an unusual situation," I explained. "Neither I nor any of my staff had ever been in a situation like that with A1C Stover. The first sergeant told me that we had to get Stover's attention because he was 'doing his own thing' in the squadron. Stover wasn't listening to his supervisors. He was caught by one of the NCOs in the first sergeant's office opening and closing his desk drawers. When asked what he was doing, he said he was looking for information for the academy's inspector general. I also learned that Stover was leaving work whenever he wanted to, questioning people about me, and telling others in the squadron that he was working for the inspector general and that he was an OSI agent." (OSI stands for Office of Special Investigations.)

OSI agents wear civilian clothing, investigate serious crimes, and work for a detachment commander rather than the base commander. This, in theory, gives them freedom to investigate anyone, without fear of retribution from their commander. "Stover's actions were disrupting the squadron," I added.

I stopped for a moment. "Surely you understand the requirement for 'good order and discipline' within a military unit," I offered. "I could not have Stover running amok, saying that he worked for the IG. People wanted to know his real status. Was he working for the IG or was he an OSI agent?

"Why was Stover asking whether anyone knew any dirt on the commander? By whose authority was he taking these actions? Stover obviously felt that he had carte blanche to do whatever he wanted," I said.

"The first sergeant brought Stover to see me and I chewed him out. I was upset that he felt he did not have to follow orders from his supervisors like everyone else in the squadron, or like everyone else in the military, for that matter. 'If you don't get in line I will see your damn ass out of the front gate,' I told Stover. That was the only time I have ever used profanity with my troops in twenty-one years as an Air Force officer."

As I finished describing the incident I realized that something was very wrong. Not only that, but the timing could not have been worse. "I am leaving tomorrow morning to visit my brother John in Maryland," I explained. "He has prostate cancer. Both of my parents died of cancer. John's wife and children are having a big birthday party for him, and my sisters and their families will be joining me in Maryland to give him moral support."

He didn't react. "Thank you, Joe. That will be all."

Apparently our "meeting" was over. During our entire conversation the academy inspector general's investigating officer had not written down a single word. He had a yellow legal pad and pen arranged on his desk and read his questions from the legal pad, but never noted any of my responses.

Our meeting had lasted about ninety minutes. I returned to my office, called in my operations officer and first sergeant and told them about the conversation. None of us was overly concerned. I was not made aware that I was the subject of an inspector general complaint. We thought that once the new chief of staff obtained the facts and realized that Stover was troubled and not performing his duties as required, this would be over.

Still, the whole encounter felt very strange. All of the questions that he asked were personal, about me. I asked myself why the academy inspector general's investigating officer was asking me about my personal actions and why some of the questions concerned things that happened two to three years ago, even before A1C Stover was in the Air Force. As a squadron commander, I had airmen make inspector general's complaints before, but they were about squadron policies that they did not agree with, such as not being able to change flights or take leave at a certain time. None were personal against me, as this one seemed. Enough doubt lingered in my mind that the next day I told Ruby, on the way to Maryland, that the USAF Academy inspector general's investigating officer had questioned me. She was surprised, too, but didn't worry much about it.

CHAPTER 3

LIES AND DECEPTION

My sojourn in Maryland was a difficult one. My brother John's fiftieth birthday was on March 21, 1984, and it was a bittersweet day, in light of his cancer. I had always admired him but, with our seven-year age difference, we had never been close. Now I feared that I would lose him to the same disease that had claimed my parents.

On my second day in Maryland I received a frantic phone call from my operations officer that the USAF Academy inspector general's investigating officer was questioning members of the squadron about me, based on an inspector general complaint by A1C Stover. "Were you aware that there was an IG complaint against you?" he asked.

"No," I replied emphatically. "The investigating officer never informed me of an IG inquiry or said he was going to question members of my squadron." It was completely unprofessional to wait until a commander was away on personal leave and then question members of his squadron. But what could I do? I was more than 1,500 miles away with my sick brother. I knew I had done nothing wrong. "Captain, can you hold down the fort until I return?" I asked. "I'll deal with this then."

A family picture from my brother's birthday party, March 1984. Front row (l-r): sisters Sadie, Gloria and Annie. Back row: me and my brother, John.

The next day I was shocked when the captain phoned again. "Colonel H., it's getting bad," he said, his voice revealing deep concern.

"What do you mean?" I asked.

"The investigating officer is cursing and yelling at the troops if they don't give him the answers he wants."

"What?" I asked, dumbfounded.

"Yeah, Colonel H., something funny is going on down here. I think they are after you."

"After me?" I asked. "But I haven't done anything."

"I know, but Colonel H., something big is happening. This isn't a normal IG. He wants certain answers. Specific answers. He even yelled at me because I would not give him the answers he wanted. Man, was he pissed," the captain continued.

Now I knew the situation was grim. The USAF Academy inspector general's investigating officer never mentioned questioning members of my squadron, even though as commander I should have been informed. Looking back now I see that the people who plotted against me had the whole thing planned out in advance. They intentionally questioned members of my squadron while I was away with my brother, thinking they could intimidate the squadron members into giving untruthful and incriminating evidence against me.

"Okay, Captain," I replied. "I'll get back to the academy as soon as I can."

A few days later I got another call from him. "Colonel H., some of the troops were so pissed at the way the inspector general's investigating officer treated them that they went to see the chief of staff. He told the NCOIC of pass and registration to get out of his office."

"What?"

"The chief of staff told him to get out, that he did not want to hear anything good about Colonel Hoffler."

Stunned, I stared into the phone. I had hoped that whatever issues he had, at least Chief of Staff Smith would handle the situation fairly. I could not have been more wrong.

Meanwhile my brother's condition stabilized. As a family we convinced John to begin cancer treatments, and eventually to have surgery. It was incredibly stressful, having to deal with his illness and the USAF Academy investigating officer situation at the same time. I could not believe how much had happened at the academy while I was in Maryland. I was only away for five days, yet my whole world had been turned upside down.

On the flight home I told Ruby what was going on and explained it the best that I could, because I did not know the whole story myself. I knew only that the investigating officer was questioning members of my squadron based on a single complaint by a troubled airman. At that point, I still believed that once I returned and talked to the new chief of staff, everything would be all right.

When I returned from Maryland I was greeted by some of the NCOs and airmen who had been interviewed by the academy's investigating officer. All of them complained about the style and substance of his questioning.

"Just wait it out and we will see what happens," I advised the men. Of special concern to me was what I heard from the Security Police Squadron's supply NCOIC. The academy's investigating officer had threatened him with disciplinary action unless he gave a written statement saying that he had given me a usable piece of Plexiglas that had some monetary value.

"Colonel Hoffler, I told him the truth," the supply NCOIC explained. "The Plexiglas I gave you was junk. I gave the investigating officer a true statement, not the statement he wanted. In my sworn statement I said that the piece of Plexiglas I gave you was approximately eighteen by twenty inches and that it was a scrap piece. I couldn't use it for anything; I probably would have thrown it out when I cleaned up the office." He paused. "Colonel, they are out to get you. I could tell based on the investigating officer's voice and questioning. They are getting all of this stuff from A1C Stover's investigation. I think they want to charge you with 'theft of government property' and give you a serious disciplinary action."

"What?" I asked in amazement.

"Colonel, the investigating officer wanted me to 'burn you.' They are trying to relieve you of command." The Security Police Squadron's supply NCOIC's words echoed my own growing concern.

"Sergeant, when did you give me that Plexiglas?" I asked.

He thought for a moment. "Last October. I remember because I was cutting off a piece for the break room. So about seven months ago," he said. "Man, they are really digging for things, aren't they?"

"Yes, they certainly are."

A week went by and I hoped that perhaps the whole thing had blown over. Then one day the day shift flight chief and the security police investigator, two black airmen, walked into my office and asked if they could speak with me.

"Of course," I replied. "What's on your minds?" I had known the day shift flight chief since 1968, when he first entered the Air Force. In fact, I had been his first commander at RAF Greenham Common in England. The security police investigator was very sharp and hardworking.

"Sir, do you know what this investigation is all about?" the flight chief asked.

"What do you mean, Sergeant?"

He shifted awkwardly. "Sir, some of the white troops are trash-talking, saying they're going to take their squadron back. This investigation isn't about a worthless piece of Plexiglas or football office pools. It's all about them 'taking their squadron back.'" His candor surprised me. "Go on," I said.

"Sir, some of the white troops don't like having a black commander to begin with. And now that the squadron has two brothers, master sergeants of the NCOIC security police operations and the NCOIC investigation, some whites in the squadron don't like that either."

I replied, "But the next in command is the captain, who is my operations officer, and he's white," I argued. "And the chief, the senior NCO, is white, too."

He nodded. "True, but your secretary and the day shift flight chief are black; that's too many blacks in senior positions for some of them. The chief is behind all of this. He is friends with Chief Church. And Chief Church worked for Chief of Staff Smith when he was director of personnel." He paused. "Sir, do you know the names of squadron personnel who the academy inspector general's investigating officer interviewed? Colonel, were you aware that he did not swear in any of the witnesses or advise them of their rights as required by Air Force regulations? That is Investigations 101. Sir, this is not an investigation; this is a witch hunt."

"No," I replied. "I'm trying to stay away and let the investigation run its course."

"Colonel, the investigating officer did not question any black security policemen, only the whites. It's like we have no voice at all. We have a commander who is approachable, respected, and fair to everyone, and some of the white airmen don't like it. A1C Stover asked for an investigation of you and he can't even qualify for duty. It just doesn't seem right, sir." Before I could respond, he continued. "Then Stover's buddy, A1C Metz, is telling everyone in the squadron that he and the chief of staff go to the same church and that he is Chief Smith's babysitter. And if anyone wants Lieutentant Colonel Hoffler gone, just let him know and he'll tell the chief of staff. There is racism throughout this whole mess, but you just can't see it, sir. What can the black troops do to support you?"

"I'm not sure," I admitted, letting the details sink in.

"We can't talk to Chief Smith, we can't talk to the IG because Stover says that he's working for him. We can't go to Social Actions because the officer there is afraid of the chief of staff," he argued passionately. "Sir, the Air Force Academy isn't an Air Force base, it's a plantation."

His analogy struck me deeply with its implication that blacks toiled at the academy as nothing more than slaves. Had I really given more than 21 years of my life for this?

"Colonel, if this can happen to a black commander, where does that leave the rest of us?" he argued. "I'm sorry, sir, but if this is how it's gonna be, I never want to work for a black commander again. I know that this would not be happening if Stover was a brother and the commander was white."

"Sergeant, I guess you are right," I replied.

After the security police investigator and the day shift flight chief left, I called in my secretary. I asked her to tell the captain and the first sergeant that I needed to see them and that I wanted her to be in the meeting also. I could read the surprise in her eyes. "You want me to stay, sir?" she asked.

"Yes, I want you to stay," I replied.

"Why, sir?" "Because I need a black airman's feel of this investigation," I explained. "For my own self-dignity, I need to confirm or deny their comments."

In the meeting that followed I shared with the captain, the first sergeant, and my secretary what they had told me. To my amazement, none of them looked surprised. I asked my secretary point blank, "Do the black troops feel that they are being ignored and that this investigation is all about race?"

"Yes, sir," she replied. "Not only black airmen in the squadron, but the word is out all over the academy that they want you removed because you are black. Everyone knows that Stover is a 'little shaky.' To have him 'dig up dirt' on you is unbelievable. Colonel, you know that the academy's investigating officer did not question any black security policemen about this case, right?"

"I know now," I replied. "I purposely stayed away. I did not want to know who he was interviewing."

"Colonel, if he was being fair, he would have questioned blacks and whites, not just the people Stover recommended or the ones he thinks will give bad stuff against you."

I turned to the first sergeant and asked him what he thought about the situation. He cleared his throat. "Sir, I am trying to believe that the actions against you are not racial. However, all of the evidence points in that direction. For example, it's hard to believe that you are being charged with betting with a staff sergeant, an enlisted person. The staff sergeant is upset because he feels that he caused the problem. He wants to tell the academy's investigating officer that it wasn't a bet. However, Colonel, the investigating officer only wants to hear one side of the story. Sir, you know I bowl. During intramural bowling, all teams have beer frames—in other words, betting that each bowler can knock down more pins than his or her teammates. Why doesn't the chief of staff charge those commanders with betting with their enlisted men who can knock down the most bowling pins?"

"First Shirt," I responded, using an affectionate term for "first sergeant," "I can't answer that question, but it's a very good comparison."

Then the captain reached into his uniform pocket, pulled out a ballpoint pen and said, "Colonel H., I wonder how many people on the academy took one of these U.S. government ballpoint pens home last night. Is the chief of staff going to charge them with stealing government property, too?"

"I doubt it, I really doubt it," I replied.

"Colonel H., I cannot figure this thing out," he said, shaking his head. "If you were a new supervisor, like Chief of Staff Smith is, having been on the job for less than two weeks, would you make an extraordinary effort to fire your most experienced commander? One who had just received an outstanding evaluation from a three-star general? Someone that HQ Military Personnel Center has asked to extend his tour? Someone who has a good chance of being promoted to colonel? If it were me, I would be begging you to extend."

"Captain, you'd think so," I said. "However, it has become obvious that the chief of staff's only objective is to replace me with someone who is white. He obviously doesn't care about job performance or experience, just ridding the academy of black officers. So far he is three for three; to use a baseball term, he is 'batting a thousand.' Two female black officers who worked for him when he was the director of personnel curtailed their assignments here at the academy and he could only supervise me for ten days before he started actions that curtailed my days as a commander."

The captain then revealed that he had been stopped by the USAF Academy inspector general in the hallway in the command building and was told, "Captain, stay out of it; we only want Joe."

"What? When?" I asked.

"Yesterday, Colonel H.," he replied.

I could not believe what I was hearing. "Do any of you feel that the chief might be involved?" I asked. The first sergeant said no.

My secretary said that she did not have any proof, but given the chief's feelings about blacks in senior positions, she would not be surprised if he was involved.

The captain spoke up. "Colonel H., I think that Chief Michaels is behind this whole investigation."

"Why do you think that?" I asked.

"Sir, a few months ago, he asked me to come into his office," the captain recalled. "He closed the door and told me, 'We've got to do something because they are taking over.'"

"Who are 'they?'" I asked. "What did he mean?"

"He said the blacks," the captain replied. "There are too many blacks in high positions in this squadron." I told him that I couldn't believe what I was hearing from a chief master sergeant in the Air Force, and that if he did not cut it out, I was going to tell you, Colonel H." The captain added, "I did not tell you then because I did not want to create a rift between blacks and whites in the squadron."

"Well, Captain, you had good intentions," I told him, "however, from what I am hearing here today, there already is a serious rift between blacks and whites."

"Colonel H., a few days after the new chief of staff assumed his office, I saw Chief Michaels coming out of his office."

"Why was the chief visiting the new chief of staff?"

"He said he was talking to Chief of Staff Smith about writing up a new pet regulation for the academy. He seemed nervous and I now know that he was lying," he continued.

"Then, sir, during the investigation, a patrol saw Chief Michaels coming out of the building where the academy's investigating officer was doing his investigation. He really had no official business in the cadet area. I imagine he gave 'evidence' against you. I did not ask him what he was doing in the cadet area. It didn't matter; he would have lied anyway." The captain shook his head sadly.

My main concern about what the captain said had to do with the chief's rank. "Chief" is a shortened form of "chief master sergeant," which is the highest enlisted rank. Chief master sergeant is a rank of high respect within the Air Force and someone with this rank is normally a leader of the squadron among the enlisted members and respected by officers. Someone of this rank wouldn't usually stab a commander in the back. That had to explain why Chief Michaels was sneaking around and meeting with Chief of Staff Smith and the academy inspector general's investigating officer. He did not want it known that he was participating in racial incidents.

I had never even been informed that I was under investigation but, at that point, I could no longer ignore that the actions against me were racially motivated. Although we were on the same staff for a few years (he as the director of personnel and as the director of security police), I barely knew Chief of Staff Smith and had done nothing to deserve this treatment. My only "crime" was being black. I had to fight his actions. However, I wondered if now I was ill equipped for such a task because I had been brainwashed to believe that everyone in the Air Force was treated fairly when it came to race and that there weren't any more old hard-line racists still around.

So I would need to reach back to the days of my youth, to a time when fighting discrimination was an everyday occurrence. I called the captain back to my office and we had a heart-to-heart talk.

I told him that I believed that the actions against me were 100 percent race-based. I had had an outstanding performance report endorsed by a three-star general only ten days before this investigation started. Meanwhile A1C Stover, who had a below average performance record at best and who had told documented lies about his personal and military life, was deemed more credible than I was by the academy's chief of staff and inspector general.

It became obvious that the investigating officer had only spoken to me in person so he could later claim I had lied. He clearly did not believe a word I said while every charge that A1C Stover made against me was deemed true and punishable, even though alleged "dirt" that he dug up, in some cases, was more than three years old. "This certainly doesn't pass the 'everyone is equal' test," I told the captain. "Stover's statements are believed because, in order to demonize me, Chief of Staff Smith and the inspector general need them to be. Surely they knew that to ask a young airman to 'dig up dirt' on his commander was unprofessional at best. And then to use that false information against a commander is beyond belief. But they had to find some reason, no matter how incredible, to put something negative in my military record and therefore deny me my command and promotion. There's no way I can get promoted to full colonel with a recent letter of reprimand in my file. The details in the letter aren't important. What's important is the effect on my career."

However, with the letter of reprimand in my personnel file, not only could I never get promoted to colonel, I could also never receive a good assignment. Having been a personnel officer, the chief of staff really knew how to end my career. Nothing I could have done could have overcome the negative impact of that unsupported letter of reprimand. As a regular Air Force officer, I could have stayed another eight years in the Air Force. However, I could not continue my Air Force career under the conditions of just receiving a paycheck and not competing for promotion.

The captain was silent as my words sank in. I still couldn't believe it. Here I was at the United States Air Force Academy, an institution that lived by, and required its cadets to live by, an honor code that said, "I will not lie, cheat, or steal or tolerate anyone among us who do." If a cadet violated that honor code, he or she was subject to punishment, even possible expulsion, from the academy. "Captain…" My voice was heavy. "How could senior officers at the academy, including the chief of staff, the inspector general, and a cadet group commander, violate the sacred honor code?"

He shook his head. "I don't know, Colonel H. I just don't know."

CHAPTER 4

SEARCHING FOR STRENGTH

I looked at the captain sitting across from me, his dark eyes full of sorrow. "I don't get it, Colonel H." He shook his head. "Racism is the only possible explanation for the chief of staff disciplining you, destroying your outstanding military record. I just can't believe he would stoop so low."

Although the captain and I had developed a close friendship, I was still his commander and there were certain personal issues that we had never discussed; I struggled to maintain the professional relationship between us. But perhaps now the time had come to delve into my past and help him understand where I came from.

"Captain, I grew up in the South," I began.

He nodded. "North Carolina, right?"

"Yes. And as a black youth growing up in the South in the 1950s and '60s, I learned a lot about what prejudice can do to people's lives."

"How bad did it get, Colonel H.?" His face was sympathetic.

"Captain, some of the things you probably wouldn't even believe."
We sat back in our chairs and I unwound my family's history, explaining

31

a black man's position in life and why I had to fight this blatant case of racism.

I was born Joseph Wood Hoffler, the youngest of six children, in Brooklyn, New York, in 1940. My father, Charles Ford Hoffler, was from Perquimans County in North Carolina and my mother, Pattie Wood Hoffler, was from Hertford, the county seat of Perquimans County. The Yeopim Indians named the area Perquimans, which means, " the land of beautiful woman.". My dad's family owned their own farmland, which they farmed, in the county. My mother's family was a prominent and well-known black family associated with the historic First Baptist Church in Hertford. Preceding the Emancipation Proclamation in 1863, fifty-eight slaves held memberships in the white church, Hertford Baptist Church, which would have been virtually unheard of at the time. Once these slaves professed their faith in the Lord they were sometimes allowed to sit in the church's balcony and participate in the worship service. The white members of this church also allowed their black brethren to use the basement of the church for services with their own black pastor ministering to them.

He stopped me. "Wait a minute, Colonel H. You mean slaves went to a white church in the 1860s?"

"Yes."

He shook his head. "Man, that is unbelievable."

This agreement for sharing the church continued until the black pastor became more politically active and began using the church building for political meetings. At that point the white church leaders stopped allowing the black members to worship there. Undaunted, this intrepid group of Christians constructed a bush shelter on Academy Square in Hertford. On June 4, 1866, services at this new church began, according to *History of First Baptist Church, 110th Anniversary Celebration, 1866-1976,* by Alberta Eason and Elizabeth Hines.

After five years the congregation needed a new place to worship. In 1871 my great-grandfather, Isaac Wood, was one of four black residents of Hertford who purchased the land for the First Baptist Church. This church is very significant in my family's history as my great-grandfather, Isaac Wood, my grandfather, John Wood, and my father, Charles F. Hoffler, were all, at one time or another, deacons and trustees in this church. My mother kept her family name, Wood, alive by giving it to me as my middle name and I passed it along to my daughter, Patricia Wood. My mother used to tell us that her family had been free black people. During those days there was no way to confirm her story. School history books in the 1950s did not teach any black history, other than the accomplishments of George Washington Carver and Booker T. Washington, so most people thought that all blacks in the South were descended from slaves. Only years later did I read in the book *The Historic Architecture of Perquimans County, North Carolina,* by Dru Gatewood Haley and Raymond Winslow, Jr., which documented incidents of free blacks living in Perquimans County. Of special note to me was the listing on page 174 of a picture of a house with the description, "a one-story coastal cottage in Hertford was probably built for Edy Wood, a freedwoman who owned the property in 1832." So it looked like my mother had been right all along!

I could see the gleam in the captain's eyes as he listened intently to my family history. Like many white Americans, he didn't realize the impressive social and cultural heritage that so many African-Americans can lay claim to.

"Tell me more," he implored, so I continued.

"My parents had six children: three girls—Annie, Sadie and Gloria—followed by three sons—Charles, John and me. The first five children were born in Hertford, North Carolina. After the birth of my brother John in 1933, my father moved the family north to Brooklyn, New York, in hopes of improving their standard of living. Many blacks in the South made this journey north in the 1930s, and that is how I came to be born in Brooklyn in 1940.

"After awhile, Brooklyn wasn't a good fit for my family anymore, so in 1945 my dad and mom decided to move back to their native North Carolina, timing the move so that I could start the first grade at my new school in Hertford, North Carolina, in 1946. My dad moved the family to Portsmouth, Virginia, which was about two hours from Hertford. In the interim, my dad and sister Sadie began working in the Navy ship-building yard in Portsmouth, Virginia. My oldest sister, Annie, stayed in Brooklyn with her husband, whom she had recently married. The youngest sister, Gloria, moved to North Carolina with us. All of my sisters finished high school in Brooklyn and later in life retired as New York City employees.

"Education was a high priority to my parents. My two brothers and I all completed high school in Hertford. Upon graduating, the eldest, Charles, received a scholarship to Winston-Salem Teachers College in Winston-Salem, North Carolina, where he attended for a year before enrolling in North Carolina College at Durham (now North Carolina Central University). Two years later, in 1953, the Army drafted him. After completing his military obligations, Charles returned to North Carolina College and earned a Bachelor of Science degree in chemistry. He went on to work in the U.S. Patent Office in Washington, D.C., and enrolled in law school at George Washington University. It was an enormous tragedy when he was killed in an auto accident in 1957. He was twenty-seven at the time; I was only sixteen.

"My brother John, seven years my senior, was also a shining star. John graduated from high school at sixteen and received an academic scholarship to Morehouse College in Atlanta, where he attended for one year. My mom, though, worried about John being so far from home at such a young age. So after his first year at Morehouse, he transferred to North Carolina College for a year before joining the Air Force. Following a four-year stint in the Air Force, he enrolled at Howard University, in Washington, D.C. John graduated from Howard with a Bachelor of Science degree in electrical engineering and worked for the Department of the Navy [until he died of cancer in 1987, the same cancer that was already ravaging him in 1984 when I went to visit him for his birthday]. Clearly, education was valued in my family. My mother was a college graduate, as were her brother and sisters. Imagine four young blacks graduating from college in the 1920s in the South; that's how far back advanced education goes in my mother's family.

"My dad was born in 1898 in Chowan County, North Carolina, and was raised by his maternal grandparents after his mother died while giving birth to him. My father was a very bright and gifted man who had only an eighth-grade education. He explained that this was because he lived in the country and there were no buses to take the black kids into town to attend high school. I have always been very proud of my dad's accomplishments. He was a self-taught auto mechanic and a business owner. My maternal grandfather was the town's blacksmith and he also owned his own blacksmith's shop, which would have been rare for a black man in those days. In fact, this was how my mother and father first met. My dad worked as my grandfather's assistant. My dad used to tease my mom by telling us, within earshot of her, that she used to visit her dad's blacksmith's shop just to flirt with him.

"My dad, who loved cars, opened his auto shop in Brooklyn and then moved it to Hertford when our family moved south. Dad eventually moved his auto shop into our backyard, about thirty yards behind our house. It was wonderful having him so close to home!" I stopped telling my story and looked at the captain.

"Your family sounds wonderful," he said. "Really smart and supportive. Strong values."

"That's right," I agreed. "Those values helped get us through the bad times."

Hertford had one bowling alley, where blacks were only allowed to work as pinsetters and, like most southern towns, had segregated schools, restaurants, a movie theater, and a monument in the courthouse yard honoring white Confederate soldiers. However, unlike most southern towns, Hertford also had a monument in a park across the street from First Baptist Church honoring colored soldiers who fought on the Union side during the Civil War. There is an inscription on a stand beside the

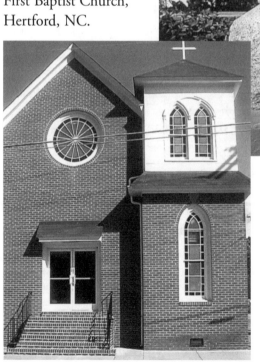

Hertford's monument in memory of the colored Union soldiers who fought in the war of 1861-1865.

First Baptist Church, Hertford, NC.

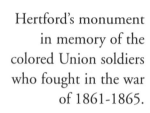

monument that states, "To remember the county's African American Union Soldiers, women of the black community, many of them wives and widows of those men, erected one of few such monuments in the nation on Academy Green." And on the monument is inscribed, "In memory of the colored Union soldiers who fought in the War of 1861-1865. N.C. Civil War Trails."

"Captain, I am very, very proud of my hometown. To think that black soldiers from my county, Perquimans County, fought with the Union Army during the Civil War. My paternal great-grandfather, Thomas Gordon, was among those troops."

Relations between the races were generally friendly. My dad had many white customers who needed to get some welding done or their vehicles repaired. He had the latest welding equipment, and I loved watching him weld, a skill he had learned in the Navy Yard while building ships. He would pull the helmet and glass visor down over his head and sparks would fly. He looked like a spaceman when he was welding!

When we lived in Hertford, Dad did all of the repairs for Jackson's Wholesale trucks and many repairs for Joe Towe's Chrysler dealership. While Dad was working or afterwards, he and the customers would sit around his shop and talk about baseball and other things. I loved listening to the stories about old times while I helped by handing Dad his tools or running errands. Looking back from the perspective of 1984, I could see that Hertford had been a typical segregated small southern town during my youth. The population was approximately 2,000, about fifty-three percent white and forty-seven percent black. There were no "other" racial categories in Hertford during the 1950s. Everyone was classified as either black or white.

But there were other options for entertainment. Every Saturday my friends and I went to the movies to see a Western. Westerns were always shown on Saturdays. Hertford had only one movie theater and the blacks sat upstairs and the whites sat downstairs. This did not bother us when we were kids; it was how things were. I certainly never felt that sitting upstairs made me inferior to the white kids sitting down below.

There was only one major restaurant in Hertford and it served only whites. I don't recall this restaurant posting a sign on its door saying, "Whites Only." There was no need. As a black person in the 1950s you just knew. Hertford, like many small southern towns, had a "black" side of town with a school, cafés and places to socialize. From the first through the third grades, I attended Hertford High School, which, despite its name, actually included grades one through twelve.

Hertford High School was the pride of Hertford's black population. Hertford High School for blacks and Perquimans County High School for whites were located nearly side by side, separated by a five-foot ditch. The contrast in the two schools was really striking. Perquimans County High was a large two-story brick building with a fenced-in, lighted yard for night baseball and football games. The school's main claim to fame is that it's the alma mater of baseball's great Jim "Catfish" Hunter, who went from Perquimans County High School straight to the Major Leagues. Hertford High for black students, on the other hand, was a single-story wooden building. Definitely separate, and definitely not equal. We always got the old textbooks, while the white students received the new textbooks.

Until the early 1950s, Perquimans County had two black high schools: Hertford High and Perquimans Training School in Winfall, which was across the river, two miles away. In the early 1950s, the county board tore down Hertford High School, built a new elementary school out of brick and named it King Street Elementary School. This school went from grades one through eight. They also built a new brick "high" school in Winfall named Perquimans County Union School. The black population of Hertford could not understand why the school board built a new high school in a smaller town rather than in the county seat of Hertford. Of course, in 1950, there were no blacks on the school board to cast a vote on where to locate their new school.

Even with the serious inequalities, growing up in Hertford in the 1950s was wonderful. Perquimans County Union School's graduating class of

1958 totaled twenty-eight students, including me. In a community so small, close friendships develop. To this day I have friends in Hertford with whom I attended the first grade, Mildred Grey, Hattie Sharpe, and Doris Brothers Felton. We are still very close and have a great time together when I visit home. My best friend in elementary school and high school was Thomas "skeet" Sharpe. Skeet lived in the county and we met in the 6th grade and were inseparable until graduation. We were captains of the varsity football and basketball teams our sophomore through senior years in school. Skeet married his high school sweetheart, Hattie James, now Hattie Sharpe.

"Captain, can you believe that my first job was driving a school bus?"

He looked surprised. "You drove a school bus?"

I laughed. "It's true," I said. "In the 1950s, students drove the school buses in North Carolina. The pay was $25 a month, and I only picked up black students. Even in the rural areas when blacks and whites lived next door to each other, they still took separate buses." He shook his head. "It's funny," I said to him, "but when I took my driving test for the school bus, I had never driven a stick shift before, only an automatic. So there I was on the bus with four or five other student drivers and when it was my turn to drive, I did the old herky-jerky routine. I couldn't get that accelerator and clutch working together." The captain and I both laughed as I pantomimed riding in a standard shift vehicle with a new driver. "I can laugh about it now but I was really embarrassed at the time," I admitted to him.

"Everyone else passed the driving test except me. When I told my dad, he was very upset. I had failed, and he didn't like the word 'failure.' To me, a sixteen-year-old kid, it was nothing but a driving test, but to my dad it was part of preparing for adulthood. He immediately took me driving in a car with a standard transmission that he had in the yard. I passed the driving test the second time I took it. But I never forgot that experience and my dad's message not to take failure lightly."

I smiled at the recollection of my dad's "tough love."

"Is that why you see not making colonel a failure?" the captain asked carefully.

I was struck by his insight. "Captain, it's deeper than that. You see, I wasn't prepared for driving a standard transmission so I failed the test. Just like I wasn't prepared for a racist supervisor like the chief of staff, so I failed to get a promotion."

"Colonel H., there was nothing you could have done to prepare for an officer like the chief of staff," he insisted.

Talking about my father brought back a lot of memories. When I was growing up, my father's heroes were Booker T. Washington and George Washington Carver. Dad would talk about them and instill in us a sense of pride, and a fierce belief that we were as good as anyone else, no matter what the color of their skin. Whenever possible my father shielded us from discrimination. For example: When I was growing up, Hertford did not have a black doctor or dentist. Our family doctor, Dr. Brinn, had segregated seating areas in his waiting room. The black patients sat on one side of the room, the white patients on the other. But Dr. Brinn examined both groups in the same examination room.

Our local dentist not only had separate waiting rooms for blacks and whites, he used separate dental chairs and instruments for his black patients. My dad was outraged and would not let us visit that particular dentist, no matter how bad our tooth ached. Instead he took us to the dentist in Edenton, about thirteen miles away. The dentist there was white but he used the same chair and instruments for black and white patients. This made a big difference to my dad and it was clearly worth the extra travel and hassle in order to receive the fair and equal treatment that we deserved.

When I turned sixteen, I started spending summers with my sisters, working in Brooklyn. However, during the summer of 1960, when I was twenty, my mother's cancer spread throughout her body and the doctors did not expect her to survive. My dad advised me not to go to Brooklyn but to stay close to home for the summer. One of my friends got me a summer job as a dishwasher in a hotel in Virginia Beach, Virginia. Virginia Beach was only about an hour and a half from Hertford so I usually came home on Sunday nights and left again early

Monday mornings. The hotel cook lived near Hertford, so we would come home every Sunday after dinner and leave on Monday, getting back in time to prepare breakfast at the hotel.

After two weeks of working at this hotel, the owner told me to go to the local police station and get a photo ID. This seemed strange, but I didn't say anything until the next time I went home. I told my dad about having to get a photo ID and he said, "No, Joseph. Absolutely not. You are not going to work at a job that requires you to have a picture ID because you are colored." The photo ID was necessary for black employees because if the police stopped a black person in the white part of town or on the boardwalk, the black person could show that he or she worked on the "Beach" and was not just out sightseeing or cruising in the white area of Virginia Beach.

Such a practice reminded me of Apartheid in South Africa, where blacks had to have passes to enter the white parts of the city. In 1960, Virginia's beaches were segregated, with Virginia Beach for the whites and a separate beach, Seaview Beach, for blacks. I wanted to continue working at the hotel because anything was better than watching my mom die a slow, painful death, but there was no way that I was going to defy my dad. I promised him that I wouldn't get a photo ID badge. So I went back to Virginia Beach for a few more weeks and before the hotel owner could ask me if I had my badge or before a policeman could ask for my photo ID, my mother's condition grew worse. I stayed home to be with her until she passed away.

I was curious about the captain's reaction to the story I had been telling him, so I momentarily stopped and looked at him. "Your parents sound like wonderful people," he said, nodding. "If anyone could possibly be prepared for the fight you're facing, it's you, Colonel H."

CHAPTER 5

ENLISTING
IN THE AIR FORCE

I started college at North Carolina College at Durham (now North Carolina Central University) in 1958 and roomed with my high school classmates, Chester Mallory and Joe Willie Skinner. Chester Mallory later became a psychology professor at Alabama State University and the owner of Mallory Real Estate Company in Montgomery, Alabama. Joe Willie Skinner retired from the State of Virginia Department of Social Services and went on to own a counseling agency. He now resides in Richmond, Virginia. We came a long way since our first arrival on the campus of North Carolina College in the fall of 1958, as three nervous freshmen from a small town. We arrived in Durham on the same Trailway bus with each of us caring all of our belongs in one suitcase. After reaching the bus station, we took a taxi to the campus. I can remember us sitting in the resident director's office waiting for our room assignments. When the director left the room, Joe Willie (Skin) and I suggested to Chester (Chet) that he ask the director could we live in the same room. Chet never bashful for words, asked the director and he said yes and assigned us a room on the freshman floor of Chidley Hall. This was the only male dormitory on campus. What a relief, that we were not going to be split up. We were roommates for our four years at NCC. We were very, very close. Initially the three us were going to major in biology, me because I was interested in the medical field and all of us had a 'crush' on our 9th grade biology teacher in high school. After biology 101, Chet decided that biology wasn't for him and Chet changed his major to psychology. However, Joe Willie and I stayed with biology, with a minor in health education.

We used the 'community system' on supplies. We shared laundry detergent, toothpaste, bath soap, ect, I have not use Jergen's bath soap since 1962. Since Joe Willie and I had the same major and minor, with the except of freshman math and english, we took all of our classes together. So whenever possible, we also shared textbooks.

Although, we were very close, for some unexplainable reason, Chet, Skin and I were drawn to different join fraternities. My brother Charles while attending NCC joined Alpha Phi Alpha, my brother John was attending Howard University joined Omega Psi Phi. I liked the Q's on NCC's campus so I pledged Omega. Chet, being more on the scholastic side pledged Alpha and Skinner favored Kappa Alpha Psi.

Also in our class was my college sweetheart, June L. Harris. We called June our "homegirl" because she was from South Mills, NC, a small town approximately thirty miles from Hertford. June and I met during our senior year in high school. She played basketball for Marion Anderson High School and I played for Perquimans County Union School. Together, we decided to attend North Carolina Central University.

My first year at North Carolina College was uneventful. However, on February 1, 1960, during my sophomore year, word hit campus that students from North Carolina A&T in Greensboro, North Carolina, approximately fifty-five miles from Durham, were conducting a sit-in at Woolworth's lunch counter. Like most lunch counters, Woolworth's had an end where blacks could order takeout or stand up and eat, but we were not allowed to sit down and eat like the white patrons. A few days after the first sit-in, students at North Carolina College organized another sit-in at the Woolworth's lunch counter in Durham.

The student leader of the sit-in, Lacy Streeter, was my classmate and fraternity brother from Omega Psi Phi fraternity. Lacy was a four-year veteran of the Air Force at that time, so he was more mature than most sophomores. My roommate Chester was one of the few students on campus who had a car, so he volunteered to drive students downtown to sit in at the lunch counter. Joe Willie and I rotated taking our seats at the lunch counter and helping Chet organize the rides. Our big day came when Lacy appeared on TV's *The Today Show* to discuss the sit-ins. For a black student to appear on *The Today Show* was a big deal in 1960. In fact, most of the students cut classes to watch the show that day. The sit-in episodes were frightening. We knew that the police were not on our side and there would be no protection for us if we went to jail. We had to put up with the name-calling and jeering from the white crowds but at least none of the students were arrested. Our main concern was not getting coffee or condiments poured on our clothing. After all, we only had one good suit each for church and we wanted to keep it neat and tidy!

In 1962, I graduated from North Carolina College with a Bachelor of Science degree in biology. And June graduated with a degree in business administration. After spending the summer of 1962 in Brooklyn, New York, I enlisted in the Air Force on September 27, 1962. I joined the Air Force because I was classified 1A. There was a military draft in 1962 and I did not want to get drafted. My eldest brother, Charles, had been in the Army in the early 1950s when it was segregated. I remembered that all of his Army pictures were with only other black soldiers. That concerned me because I wasn't sure how much progress the Army had made in the area of integration. My other brother, John, had served four years in the Air Force and recommended it to me. As there wasn't a war going on in 1962, my family thought my joining the military was the right thing to do and wholly supported me.

June and I became engaged in the summer of 1962, just prior to me enlisting in the Air Force. After graduation, she was hired in the business office at North Carolina Central University. I left for my military career from New York City and took my first airplane ride ever to San Antonio, Texas. I arrived at Lackland Air Force Base (AFB) in San Antonio on September 27, 1962. With few exceptions, all of the Air Force's basic training was given at Lackland AFB. During training, we studied the Air Force mission, organization, and military customs and courtesies; performed drill and ceremony marches; and received physical training, rifle marksmanship, and field training exercises. After my first six weeks in basic training, we were given our career field designations. At that time the Air Force did not guarantee that a recruit would get a specific career field, but it did guarantee that the recruit would get a job within one of four areas. Since my background and interest was biology, I signed up for the "general category," which included the areas of air police (now named security forces), medical, food service, transportation, and administrative. The "general category" was considered one of the less-technical career fields in the Air Force.

When our career field assignments were finalized, I found out that I had been selected for the air police career field. I was somewhat dejected because I had had my mind set on the medical field and hoped someday to become a doctor.

Obviously that's going to have to be put on hold for at least four years, I told myself. My training instructor (TI) said that I had been assigned to the air police career field because the Cuban Missile Crisis was going on and the Air Force needed air policemen to guard the airplanes and facilities on their bases. I accepted that the needs of the Air Force had precedence over the desires of the individual.

Soon after I received my career assignment, my basic training flight (a flight, next to a squad, is the second lowest organizational element of the Air Force) was divided into those who were chosen for technical schools and those who weren't. I was among those not chosen, so I joined the other airmen who hadn't been chosen for technical school. We were put into a new flight and moved to the other side of the base while the other members went off to technical school. The rumor around the flight was that to be selected for technical school, one had to score high on the

Armed Forces Qualifying Test (AFQT). I couldn't understand this because with my degree in biology, I was certain that I had scored higher than most of the other recruits, who had completed only high school. In addition, I had seen some of those other guys struggle with lessons during the first eight weeks.

Putting my frustration aside, I arrived at my new basic squadron and noticed that it was composed mostly of black airmen. For the first several weeks all we did was a little drill, play cards, pull KP or other details, and eat. None of these things required any brainpower. I began to wonder what I had gotten into. Had my brother John been in a different Air Force? Based on his recommendation I did not expect to see blacks so segregated here. It reminded me of those old World War II movies with black soldiers just "killing time" and waiting to be allowed to fight. Our flight had very little to do. However, being new to the Air Force I could not put it together at that time, but I knew that the white airmen with whom I would be competing for promotion had an advantage. They were in a classroom learning the air police career field while I was doing nothing. My assumption was correct, but the proof would not become evident until after a few months at my first assignment.

When I graduated from my twelve weeks of basic training, my first assignment as an air policeman was to Truax Field in Madison, Wisconsin. The Air Force gave me a bus and train ticket from Lackland AFB in San Antonio to Madison, Wisconsin, where I would be stationed, via Hertford, North Carolina. When I boarded the bus in San Antonio, in my Air Force uniform, I knew I would be traveling through the Deep South into North Carolina, so out of habit, I sat in the rear of the bus. As we drove out of San Antonio, Texas, I contemplated how I was going to spend the next two days on the bus. Although I had been raised in the South, my parents had always protected me from the indignity of having to eat on the "colored" side of a restaurant or from a "colored" window. When we traveled from New York to Hertford my mom always packed us a lunch, which we ate in the car.

Already onboard when I got on the bus out of San Antonio was a handful of sailors who had just completed their boot camp, the equivalent of the Air Force basic training, in San Diego. From their accents I could tell that they were Southerners, probably going home on leave. I also noticed that some of them had small Confederate flags sewn to the inside cuffs of their uniform sleeves. I thought that was strange.

I couldn't imagine the Air Force allowing us to modify our uniforms, especially to add non-Air Force items.

These sailors on leave were very loud and appeared to have been drinking. They gave the three other black airmen on the bus and me very hard stares, but they did not direct any racial comments towards us. However, I was braced for the worst. As a young adult I had always refused to patronize segregated businesses that required me to order from a side window. When I attended college in Durham, there were many black-owned restaurants near the campus so there was never any trouble finding somewhere to eat. Then whenever I traveled home from college (with Chester and Joe Willie), we always stopped to eat at a black-owned restaurant in Rocky Mount, North Carolina. But now, as I sat on that bus out of San Antonio, I was helpless. My mom wasn't around to fix me a sandwich and I couldn't ask the bus driver to stop at a black-owned restaurant. And, of course, I could not go without food for two or three days. So when the bus made its first rest stop, there I was dressed in my Air Force uniform, but I refused to get a sandwich from the "colored" window. How sadly ironic that I was forced to decide whether to eat in a segregated restaurant while wearing the uniform of the United States Air Force.

Traveling with me were three other black airmen, all younger than I. One was from Alabama and two from Georgia. At the time we were only about one year removed from the bloody Freedom Rides, in which blacks and whites attempted to integrate interstate buses. At the second rest stop, the other black airmen asked if they could bring me something to eat. I said yes and they brought me back a sandwich, which I ate while standing outside of the bus.

I just couldn't go up to that side window while the white servicemen were able to go inside, sit down and get a hot meal. I did not fault the black airmen who went to the window. I was older than they were and had experienced a different upbringing. On the contrary, I appreciated their willingness to help.

Although I was able to avoid the segregated restaurants, during the trip I had no choice but to use "colored" restrooms. I was accustomed to that because when we bought gas while traveling in the South, we had to use segregated restrooms. Some gas stations had separate white and colored restrooms. Some had only white restrooms. If in any doubt, before buying gasoline, my dad would always ask the person working, "Do you have a restroom for coloreds?" If the man said no, Dad would move on until he found a gasoline station that would allow us to use the restroom.

After two weeks' leave at home I began the trip from North Carolina to Madison. I traveled while wearing my uniform, which was required in 1962. Not only was it required but despite my experience on the trip from San Antonio to Hertford, I was proud to serve my country. I was happy to be stationed in the Midwest because I had never been out of the East Coast. I was excited to see Wisconsin and thought that perhaps I might even take some graduate courses at the University of Wisconsin. I traveled by bus as far as Chicago then boarded a train to Madison and finally a taxi to Truax Field, arriving at headquarters in November 1962. The snow on the ground that greeted me was nearly waist-high. I eagerly signed in and was given my barracks number.

Due to the Cuban Missile Crisis, there was a heavy influx of new personnel to the base, and my first few days were spent, along with two other newly arrived air policemen, in a dayroom that had been transformed into a dormitory room. The other two airmen were also black. "Bear" from Fort Worth, Texas, was a big guy, probably six-foot-three and more than 200 pounds. Youngblood, a slightly built guy from Louisiana, was only about five-foot-three and lightweight. Our first two to three weeks at Truax were spent on what the Air Force called "OJT" or on-the-job training. Since Bear, Youngblood and I did not go to technical school, our time was spent learning to be air policemen. We were required to qualify with a rifle and handgun and learn how to wear the air police uniform properly. We also learned other air police tasks such as writing traffic tickets and learning the different restricted area badges. After those initial weeks of training, Bear, Youngblood and I were assigned to different flights.

During December of 1962, all of the Air Force planes that could fly were deployed to Homestead AFB in Florida, standing alert due to the Cuban Missile Crisis. The whole DOD (Department of Defense) was in a high DEFCON (defense conditions), so we were required to work twelve-hour shifts, twelve hours on and twelve hours off. There wasn't a lot that needed guarding at Truax, but nonetheless the twelve-hour shift started my Air Force career.

Initially my assignment at Truax was tough. Walking around F-89 Scorpions from the Wisconsin National Guard, F-102 fighter aircraft, and the SAGE (semi-automatic ground environment) building all hours of the night in subfreezing temperatures was not what I had planned for my Air Force service. I had hoped to be assigned to a lab working in my chosen field of biology. However, once someone joins active duty, he or she learns quickly that the "needs of the Air Force come first." The Air Force obviously needed me to be an air policeman more than they needed me in a laboratory. Initially, I found shift work difficult as well. I had never worked night shifts before and all of a sudden having to stay awake on a midnight shift, from 2300 hours to 0700 hours, was hard. However, I was highly motivated to stay out of trouble. So I managed to sleep during the day and stay awake at night.

After a few weeks living in the dayroom, I was assigned to a barracks room. The first few days, I had the room to myself but then my two roommates arrived. Oscar Miller, affectionately known as "Moose," was from Tennessee, and Michael Cunningham was from Indianapolis. Both are white. Here I was at twenty-two years old, having my first social experience with white people. *Well*, I thought, *I'm sure that I am*

A2C Hoffler, third from the left, serving on the Truax Field Honor Guard.

the first black person they've ever associated with as well, so that makes us even. In fact, the three of us got along great. We were assigned to the same flight and working shifts, so we were all off duty at the same time.

Both Mike and Moose had been to technical school, and this meant that they were more skilled than those of us who hadn't gone. I had arrived with an AFSC (Air Force specialty code) of 77010. The key number here was one, because that indicated a person's skill level. Because Mike and Moose had gone to technical school, they arrived at Truax Field with skill levels of three. Although Bear, Youngblood and I had been in the Air Force longer than Moose and Mike, the three of us were at level 1 and the two were at level three. Their having their three level before us was very important because it meant that they could be assigned to better postings. They could get the more skilled postings such as desk sergeant, inside entry controller, stockade, armory, team leader, etc. This also meant that they were allowed to drive vehicles and never had to get out to relieve another post. Having such privileges in a cold climate like Wisconsin was important because most of the other postings were outside.

As time went on it became clear to me that things had not been equal in the selection of air policemen to attend technical school. For me and the other black airmen to earn our three levels, we would have to work and study during our off-duty time, while the white airmen went to school full-time at the Air Police Academy. There was an obvious racial bias in the selection of air police to attend technical school. None of the black airmen I knew—Wallace, Farrell, Youngblood, "Bear," or Barney— had attended Air Police Technical School; however, all of the white airmen had. In addition, being at a three level gave the white airmen an advantage when it came to promotion because air policemen were required to have a level three in order to get promoted. So while I was stuck working on my 3 level, Mike, Moose, and the other white airmen were already working on their five level.

Even so, race relations at Truax Field were generally good. We did not blame the white airmen for receiving such advantages; it was the nature of the system itself that discriminated against blacks. Then again, maybe relations were good because no one wanted to quarrel with people who were armed! I only recall one near incident on base during my time there. In this particular incident, my flight was preparing for work and there was a crowd of people in line to get our weapons from the armory. In front of me was A2C Tommy Finn. A2C Finn, who hailed from South Carolina, had just returned from leave and was talking to another white airman in line with him. Finn obviously forgot where he was and who was standing behind him, namely me.

A2C Finn told his friend, "I was on the beach and this girl had a tan; she was so dark she looked just like a nigger." The whole place got quiet. Everyone sort of looked at one another as if to say, "I don't believe what I just heard." Finn looked around and realized there were black people within earshot. Although I wasn't the senior person in rank present, I felt that something had to be done to ease the tension.

So I said, "Tommy, you do mean 'Negro'?"

He said, "Yes, Joe, that's what I meant. I'm sorry."

I said okay but two black airmen on my flight, Farrell and Wallace, turned and slowly walked away. Farrell was from Washington, D.C., and Wallace was from Detroit. Both of them outranked me.

Fortunately I had patrol that shift so that I could visit all of the posts and settle things down with Farrell and Wallace. I told them, "We know that they use that word in private; therefore, it shouldn't surprise us that Tommy slipped and used it in public. He just forgot where he was. Besides, it wasn't worth causing any trouble over. Now if Tommy had directed that comment at one of us directly, that would have been a whole different situation."

As far as I was concerned, Tommy was in his own world, talking to another white airman, and did not mean to put anyone down.

I was glad I was able to address that situation before it developed into anything worse. My flight chief later complimented me for defusing what could have been a touchy situation.

Although race relations were okay at Truax, I did have one very frightening experience off base. Sometimes my roommate Mike Cunningham would fly home to Indianapolis over his break. To get him to the airport in time, I would drive him there right after we got off from work, then pick him up when he returned to Madison two and a half days later. One day, after I dropped Mike off at the airport, Farrell, Wallace and I decided to "see" some of Madison before returning to base. While cruising around town, I noticed in my rearview mirror a policeman's car with his lights and sirens on, so I pulled over. I knew I had not run a traffic light, nor was I speeding. The policeman approached the car.

"Are you boys from Milwaukee?" he asked.

"No," I replied.

"Did you know your license tag has expired?"

"No, sir."

"Let me see your vehicle registration," he continued. I handed him the card, which showed Michael Cunningham's name. He looked at us suspiciously. "Which one of you is Cunningham?"

"Mike isn't here," I answered. "I have his permission to drive his car."

"All right, exit the car with your hands up," the officer said.

Scared, I followed his orders and positioned myself spread-eagle against the car's roof and hood. Within minutes two more police cars drove up with their lights on and sirens blazing.

"Okay, where are the guns?" the first policeman asked.

"What guns?" I replied.

He pointed to the holsters and gun belts on the back seat.

"We are air policemen from Truax Field. Those are government holsters and gun belts," I explained.

Not satisfied, the officer asked his dispatcher to check if there had been any reports of a stolen 1958 Ford, and to call the base and verify that Ferrell, Wallace and Hoffler really were assigned to the Air Police Squadron there. The air police desk sergeant confirmed that we were air policemen assigned to Truax Air Force Base. The police officers had seen the gun holsters in the back seat of the car and must have assumed that because we were black, we were going to rob a bank or something.

In 1962 Air Force personnel were not allowed to wear their fatigues off base, as they can today. So we were in civilian clothes, and since we had been in a hurry to get Mike to the airport, we had left our air police holsters on the car's back seat, never dreaming it would cause such trouble. After the incident was over the three of us came to believe that initially the policeman stopped us because he saw three black men in a car cruising Madison and decided that we were in the "wrong" part of town. The tags on Mike's car had expired. So I gave the warning ticket to him when he returned.

CHAPTER 6

SELECTED FOR OFFICER TRAINING SCHOOL

A social life was out of the question for me in Madison in 1962. Besides being engaged to June back home, working the long air police shifts of nine days on and three days off didn't leave much time for socializing. I spent most of my time at Truax working, and when I had my days off, I read or played sports. Once I decided to apply for Officers Training School (OTS), I knew that I could not afford any "write-ups" that would disqualify me for selection. So I made a special effort to keep my nose clean. Unlike many career fields in the Air Force, the air police career field provided plenty of opportunities to get written up. These included such things as being late for work, having a uniform not pressed or shoes not shined, sleeping on post, etc. I think air police was one of the few career fields that inspected their troops prior to starting work.

I had to wait a year at Truax Field before I could test for OTS, so I kept my nose clean, resisting all offers to go to Chicago, Milwaukee, Madison, or other places where I could not control the situation or the time I would return to base. I could not afford to be late. Not that the supervisors would purposely give me a write-up, but I just did not want to give them the opportunity. Fortunately, I had a black officer in charge, Lieutenant Quann, who took an interest in me because of my job performance. One cold October morning after I had worked a midnight shift, he called me into his office and told me that he heard I had a college degree in biology.

"Yes, sir," I replied proudly.

"Then why did you enlist in the Air Force rather than seek a commission and become an officer?" he asked.

I told him about my experience with the Air Force recruiter in Durham, NC, who was reluctant to give me the Air Force Officer's Qualifying Test because he said that was only for students from Duke University or, in other words, only for students who were white.

When Lt. Quann heard that story he said, "We will not have that here. Do you still want to apply for Officers Training School? You've been doing an outstanding job so I would be happy to recommend you." Having an officer endorsement was remarkable. I told him that I would apply to take the OTS test. Lt. Quann instructed the operations clerk to obtain the necessary forms and schedule a testing date for me. He wished me luck and told me to keep him posted on my progress.

So I studied, took the test, passed, and completed the paperwork for OTS. The word got around that I had passed the test and was waiting for selection. Most of the guys started calling me "Lieutenant," after a popular TV show at the time about a Marine lieutenant. The show was titled "The Lieutenant."

When I was accepted for OTS, I also received word that I was going to the Air Force Bioenvironmental Engineering School. I was thrilled to be going into my chosen field of biology. But then two weeks before I was scheduled to leave Truax, orders came down that changed my career field to air police. My friends were very happy that I was going to OTS. The squadron commander and Lt. Quann posed with me for a picture for the base newspaper. Without Lt. Quann's support, I don't think I would have made it. His support really "marked" my Air Force career in a positive way.

"I'm turning in my badge." could well have been the words of A2C Joseph W. Hoffler (center) to Maj. Eugene A. Lamar (left), Chief, Security and Law Enforcement, 327th ABRON. Airman Hoffler left Wednesday on his way to the Officers Training School, Lackland AFB. 1st Lt Byron G. Quann,(right), operations officer of the Air Police section, observes the farewell ceremony. Airman Hoffler, with sixteen months of service in the Air Force, is a graduate of the Perquimans Union High School, Hartford, NC, and hold a B.S. degree from North Caroline College. After completing the three month OTS course, Airman Hoffler expects to continue in the Air Force career field.

Like my mentor, Lt. Quann, I also tried to help other enlisted members seek Air Force commissions whenever possible. While squadron commander at RAF Mildenhall, I had two airmen complete their college degrees and be accepted into Officers Training School. While squadron commander at the academy, I had two members complete their college degrees and get accepted into OTS. Two other members were accepted into the Air Force Preparatory School, which is the route for enlisted members of the Air Force to enter the Air Force Academy as cadets. I saw my service at the academy as another way to "give back" to the military by helping young officers and airmen of all races live up to their potential. But back in the mid 1960s I had no idea that the Air Force would later repay me for my years of service by letting a racist commander and his henchmen destroy my career.

After one and a half years at Truax Field, I was back at Lackland Air Force Base in San Antonio, TX, for the second time in my career. I entered Officers Training School in April 1964 and was assigned to

Squadron 12. In my flight of eighteen officer trainees, only two of us were black: McClendon and me. McClendon also had prior service, having been in the medical career field before enrolling in OTS. In general OTS was great, but racial incidents around the country were increasing as I neared graduation. By June 1964, the country was in a civil rights upheaval and racial tensions were high, especially in the South.

At the end of June, three civil rights workers—Michael Schwerner, Andrew Goodman and James Chaney—disappeared in Mississippi while trying to register black voters.

I graduated from OTS on July 1, 1964, and planned to go home for thirty days. Unfortunately, the most direct route from San Antonio to North Carolina would take me through the Deep South via Atlanta and Durham into Hertford. I worried about getting home safely, without having to drive hundreds of miles out of my way. Two white members of my flight who lived in small towns around Atlanta volunteered to ride with me to their hometowns, as sort of an escort.

I said, "What? Three civil rights workers—two whites and one black—are missing, and now you say that the same combination will be safe driving in a new 1964 Chevrolet through Mississippi, Louisiana, Alabama and Georgia? Won't the KKK think we're civil rights workers?"

"Joe," one of them said, "we're in danger, too. Those civil rights workers are still missing."

After thinking about it, I realized that they understood they would be in as much danger as I was. "I guess you are right. Let's go for it."

One of the instructors suggested that we display our uniforms in the rear side windows and our hats in the rear window so passers-by would know that we were in the military. My passengers weren't really afraid, but I had to admit that I was. It was my first time driving through the Deep South and the prevalent racial climate made it harder.

The family of one of my passengers met us at a general store and the other asked that I drop him off at his house. When we drove up to his yard, his family came out to meet us. We shook hands and exchanged the customary greetings. They invited me in for dinner but I declined because it was getting late and I wanted to get to my next destination before dark. A black person driving alone at night in a new car during that era of civil unrest wasn't a smart thing to do. I felt that the family's dinner invitation was sincere because I knew that they knew that he was riding with me. As I left the house and drove on the road, I could feel that a car was following me. I thought to myself, *How stupid was that? Standing in the front yard of a white family and shaking their hands.* I had broken a Southern taboo. Black people never went to the front door of a white person's house. Never. Having seen me in the front yard, surely I thought the car of white men following me was determined to "put me in my place." However, the car passed me and kept on going. Maybe seeing my uniform hanging in the back window scared them off. I guess I'll never really know why they did not stop me.

In 1964, blacks could not use hotels in the South, so if you were in the military and traveling overnight, you mapped your route from military installation to military installation and spent the nights there. I spent the night at Fort McPherson's VOQ (visiting officers quarters). The next morning I traveled to North Carolina and for some strange reason, when I crossed the state line, I felt relieved. I stopped in Durham, bunking in my old dormitory with my buddies before continuing home to Hertford. After being on leave I returned to Lackland Air Force Base in Texas to begin Security Police Officers School.

After graduating from Security Police Officers School, I traveled to Shreveport, Louisiana, on my way home and stayed at Barksdale AFB the first night. My next planned stop was Fort McPherson near Atlanta. As always, I was being careful, keeping within the posted speed limit. As recommended, again I had my uniform prominently displayed in my rear driver's side window, so that anyone who stopped me would see that I was in the military. I stopped for gas only after checking that there wasn't a crowd of men sitting outside on a bench at the general store or around the gas pumps. All it would take was for one or two to ask, "Boy, where did you get that fancy car?" and things could have gotten nasty real fast.

After stopping at a store for gas and snacks in Alabama, I continued along a main two-lane road. After about five miles I looked up ahead and saw two Alabama state troopers with their cars blocking the road and waving for me to stop. My first thought was that someone at my last stop had called the police to accuse me of stealing from the store. All kinds of awful thoughts ran thought my mind, from not stopping to, 'I'll probably be on the national news.' But I was in strange territory and did not know any of the back roads so I had to stop. As I slowed down I noticed that the state trooper had a sheet of paper in his hand and I wondered what it could be. A wanted poster with my name and face on it? Anyway, as I stopped, the trooper approached my car and handed me the sheet of paper.

"Governor Wallace requests that you have a safe Labor Day weekend and drive safely."

It looked like they were stopping all drivers and issuing them handbills from the governor requesting that everyone drive safely for the holiday. Man, was I relieved as I continued on my way.

When I arrived home, June and I were married in September 1964. We had very little time for our honeymoon, as I had to soon depart for my first assignment to Griffiss Air Force Base in Rome, New York. At Griffiss, I was assigned to the 416th Bomb Wing of the Strategic Air Command (SAC) Wing, which at that time had B-52 bombers and KC-135 tankers aircraft. The unit commander was a senior captain and within three weeks of my arrival, two other second lieutenants were assigned to the unit. Steve was assigned as the operations officer, I was the security education and motivation officer and Bob was the training officer. I really enjoyed the assignment. My job was to develop lesson plans on security procedures and the protection of classified material and to instruct the wing personnel on security. I was also appointed as the squadron athletic officer. I coached and played on the squadron's flag football and basketball teams, which won the base championship.

Due to a conflict in careers, June never joined me at Griffiss AFB, and we were divorced in 1965. Socially, since there was only a small black population in Rome, we black officers usually entertained ourselves via get-togethers at people's homes. After a year at Griffiss AFB, I married my lovely wife Ruby in 1965 in Utica, New York. I originally met her in 1964 on a blind date while I was in Security Police Officers School at Lackland AFB, TX. Then she was A1C Ruby Kimbrough. Ruby was an X-ray technician stationed at Wilford Hall Hospital, Lackland AFB. After my divorce, our friendly relationship escalated into one of love. Not wanting to violate the Air Force's policy against fraternization between officers and enlisted personnel, when Ruby's enlistment was up, I asked her to come to New York to marry me and she accepted my proposal.

We met some lifelong friends while at Griffiss, including Isaac Payne. Ike, a B-52 pilot, was in the first class of blacks who graduated from the Air Force Academy in 1963. We also became friends with Charles "Chuck" and Dianne Showell, Van and Yvonne Walker, and Maxie and Maxine Harrell. Chuck and Van worked in aircraft maintenance while Maxie worked in a lab doing research. Griffiss AFB was a tough assignment for the security policemen in the Strategic Air Command. Griffiss AFB was an AFLC base and the base police law enforcement unit was made up of civilians. This meant that all of the young security policemen were given mostly outside posts, walking in front of or behind a B-52 or a KC-135 in all kinds of weather.

One very cold day, TSgt. Gaithers, a flight chief, brought a young airman into my office. "Lieutenant, this airman wants to quit," Gaithers said. "He says it's too cold to walk around airplanes all day." Unlike the other two lieutenants, I was the only officer who had been an enlisted security policeman, so I was often asked to deal with situations in which security policemen wanted to quit their posts due to having to stand outside in the harsh weather conditions.

"So why do you want to quit?" I asked the young man.

"Lieutenant, you don't know what it's like to freeze for four or five hours walking the flight line. You guys got it made in this warm office."

"Airman," I said, "do you think that you are the only security policeman who is cold? And do you think this is worth getting court-martialed for? Because that is what is going to happen if you don't return to your post."

His face sagged. "Sir, I can't take it any longer," he argued. "You don't know how it feels out there."

I pointed to a photograph of me hanging on my office wall as a member of the Truax Field Color Guard. "Take a look at this."

He looked closer. "Is that you?"

"Yes, it is."

"I didn't know that you were enlisted. What base were you at?"

"I was at Truax Field in Wisconsin and as you know, it gets very cold in Wisconsin. So, Airman, don't think for one moment that you are the only security policeman in the Air Force who's ever thought about quitting his post. That thought went through my own mind many times, but I knew I could not quit."

"Lieutenant, I am sorry," the young airman said. "I didn't know that you were prior enlisted. I'll return to my post, sir. You won't have any more trouble from me, I promise." Then he picked up his rifle, saluted and left my office.

Gaithers looked at me and winked as if to say, "I told him so." Being able to tell the young security policemen under my command that I had been in their shoes and had gone through what they were going through helped me establish a tremendous amount of credibility with them and also made my job as supervisor/commander a lot easier.

CHAPTER 7

OUR FIRST OVERSEAS ASSIGNMENT

In February 1967, I received orders to report to RAF (Royal Air Force) Bentwaters in England. This was my first assignment overseas so Ruby and I planned a trip to Memphis, Tennessee, to say goodbye to her family. We were going to be gone for a three-year tour in England, so it was important to connect with family members before we left. Knowing that my dad had watched the civil rights battles on TV, we invited him to come with us and visit Ruby's home in Memphis. From Memphis we traveled to Mississippi to visit Ruby's grandparents and on to Montgomery, Alabama, to visit my high school buddy and college roommate, Chester Mallory.

That trip was my dad's first trip into the Deep South. He really enjoyed seeing the spots where so many significant events in the civil rights battles occurred. The most striking part of our trip was our stop at the renowned Tuskegee Institute, which was founded by Booker T. Washington and was also the place where George Washington Carver had his famous laboratory. My dad was touched to see Tuskegee, a place he never believed he would see, and the sights of the many civil rights battles in the city of Montgomery, AL. I cherished having the opportunity to spend quality time with my dad, who had inspired me to compete with all I had at all times.

The 81st Security Police Squadron at RAF Bentwaters in England covered two large Royal Air Force bases, RAF Woodbridge and RAF Bentwaters. I was assigned as the operations officer, which meant that I was second in command to the commander. At RAF Bentwaters, I met my first black chief master sergeant in the security police career field, CMSgt. David Bryant. CMSgt. Bryant was from Tampa, FL. Chief Bryant was really sharp, a no-nonsense NCO and well respected among the troops. Also assigned to the squadron was a white chief master sergeant named Ed Wyatt. He hailed from West Memphis, Arkansas, across the bridge from Memphis, Tennessee. He was the senior enlisted advisor to the commander. Soon after I arrived at RAF Bentwaters I noticed that the commander's secretary, Ms. Hines, would laugh slightly as I passed by her desk on my way into or out of the commander's office. Ms. Hines is black and her husband was a well-respected first sergeant After I got to know Ms. Hines better I asked her one day why she used to laugh when I walked by her desk. She said, "Lt. Hoffler, you really fooled them."

"Fooled who?" I asked.

"The commander and his staff."

"What do you mean?"

She explained that when they initially saw my name, Hoffler, they assumed that a blond-haired, blue-eyed German had been assigned to the squadron. Then, when they saw me, they could not believe it. "It's obvious that your name confused them," she explained. "But the joke was on them."

On April 4, 1968, I was sitting in the commander's office when Chief Wyatt entered through a side door and announced, breathlessly, "I knew we would get him if he came to my part of the country."

"Who? What's going on?" Lt. Col. Gallinger asked.

"I just heard on Armed Forces Radio that Martin Luther King, Jr., was assassinated in Memphis," Chief Wyatt replied. Then he turned around and saw me sitting behind the door. He attempted to apologize but I told him an apology wasn't necessary because I knew he meant what he said the first time. Then I stood up and left Lt. Col. Gallinger's office. As far as I know, Wyatt was never disciplined for his comment.

Although I did not appreciate Chief Wyatt's comments about the death of Dr. Martin Luther King, Jr., I liked the way he performed his duties of senior enlisted advisor to the commander. He assisted enlisted personnel in the areas of testing for promotion, reenlisting, encouraging them to take college courses, and just chatting with them about anything on their minds. And I promised myself that if I ever became a squadron commander, I would duplicate the position of senior enlisted advisor to the commander. Being prior enlisted, I knew how valuable it was to have such a person in the squadron. While at RAF Mildenhall, I used SMSgt. Tom Jones for that position. I recruited the chief for that position at the USAF Academy; however, he seemed more interested in the number of blacks coming into the squadron.

After a year and a half at RAF Bentwaters, the commander called me into his office and told me that I had done such an outstanding job that he was recommending me for a "special assignment." They needed a security police officer to become the chief of security police at RAF Greenham Common in England and they needed someone who could work alone, without supervision. RAF Greenham Common had previously been a Strategic Air Command (SAC) base that was reopening. There were only ten officers on base and our main mission was to provide storage space for U.S. equipment that was being relocated from bases in France. This was a very nice assignment and I was excited by the prospect of taking it on.

The base commander at RAF Greenham Common was Colonel Ronald Dunlap, who was rumored to be a survivor of the Bataan Death March. I never asked him if this was true; however, I heard it from a credible source. He proved to be a great commander. While at RAF Greenham Common, Colonel Dunlap recommended to me that I cross train into the missile career field to get some operational experience, which would help me get promoted to major. I applied for cross training into the Minuteman missile career field and was assigned to Whiteman AFB in Missouri.

I arrived at Whiteman AFB in August 1969 and went to missile training at Vandenberg AFB in California before returning to Whiteman in January 1970. I began my missile duty as a deputy commander. My commander was Captain Al Zamora, who was very helpful in teaching me my duties and assisted me in becoming qualified to upgrade to become a missile combat crew commander. So in the minimum amount of time, I upgraded from deputy to commander. On my initial qualification evaluation, I scored a 4.9 out of a maximum score of 5.0. A score of 4.5 to 5.0 is considered "highly qualified." When I upgraded to commander I scored another 4.9. So I had had two evaluations and achieved "highly qualified" marks on both. Six months later, my crew and I had another evaluation and we scored 5.0. The missile career field at Whiteman AFB was divided into line crewmembers, instructor crewmembers and standardization crewmembers.

One day it occurred to a few of the black missile crewmembers that there were no blacks in the training and standboard divisions. So along with Lts. Ken Dollar and Tony Peguese, I met with the director of operations, Colonel Hayes. After being briefed on the situation, Col. Hayes said he would look into it. He had not noticed the lack of blacks in the training and standboard divisions. A short time later, when openings occurred in the training branch, both Lts. Dollar and Peguese were transferred into it as deputy instructors. Both lieutenants had achieved "highly qualified" ratings on all of their evaluations. A few months later I was selected as a crew commander for the instructor branch. Then I was selected to go to the standardization branch. I was the first black commander in the standboard in two years. Most importantly, I was the most qualified crew commander for that coveted position. Lts. Dollar and Peguese and I were not looking for affirmative action or to fill quotas for those positions; we were the most qualified applicants for the positions. We just wanted to be sure that when positions opened up, blacks with outstanding records were given consideration.

Performing a facility check prior to going on alert as a Minuteman Missile
Launch Crew Commander.

After a tour in the standboard branch, I was selected to upgrade to a
staff position at the codes vault, where the coding for missiles is made.
While in the codes branch, I was selected for promotion to major. At
Whiteman AFB, I obtained my MBA from the University of Missouri
via the Minuteman Missile Education Program and completed the Air
Command and Staff course by correspondence.

Then the assignment "war" began. Soon after my selection for
promotion to major in 1975, I received an assignment as an airborne missile launch officer at Ellsworth AFB, South Dakota, which was the top of
the missile career field. However, my security police career advisor informed
me that security police had priority on my assignments and that he wanted
me to stay in the security police career field. I asked, "Why me?" The early
1970s was an era of race riots and racial incidents in the military, including
the Air Force. The most notorious cases were race riots at Travis AFB in
California in May 1971 and at Laredo Air Force base in Texas in September
1972. Race relations in the military were on the front burner then.

Since the security police career field had a large percentage of black
personnel with guns, there was a concern that the career field should
retain outstanding black officers and NCOs. Therefore I was retained.

My career advisor explained that the Air Force needed me to serve as a mentor and to help in this effort, I gladly accepted the challenge. He then told me that I had to go to Southeast Asia (SEA), where he would give me an assignment as a Security Police Squadron commander, which was what I wanted. I was selected to become a squadron commander of a Security Police Squadron in Korea. However, weeks before I was due to report, while I was undergoing combat training at the Security Police Academy in Texas, the Air Force changed the assignment as the base was not designated to reopen.

I was then reassigned to HQ 13th AF ADVON at Udorn AB in Thailand, which controlled the Air Force units in that country. My supervisor, Lt. Col. Willingham, was black. Shortly before I arrived in Thailand, the Air Force began closing down bases. In addition, there were racial tensions between some black and white airmen in the Security Police Squadron at Utapo AB in Thailand. The general at 13th ADVON sent my supervisor, Lt. Col. Willingham, to Utapo to investigate the situation.

Due to the racial tension there, after a few visits, Lt. Col. Willingham was permanently assigned to the Security Police Squadron at Utapo AB.

After Udorn closed, I was assigned as the operations officer to the base security police unit at Utapo Air Base. Also assigned with me was Chief Master Sergeant Joe Canada, who was previously assigned with the base security police unit at Udorn. It was obvious to us that the Air Force transferred us to Utapo AB to provide some visibility of senior black officers and NCOs. Joe Canada and I spent a lot of time talking to the troops at Utapo. However, I think that our mere presence in the squadron provided a calming effect on the unit.

After eleven months in Southeast Asia I was transferred back to England, to RAF Mildenhall and my first assignment as a squadron commander. I was really excited about becoming a squadron commander. During those days, everyone going to England departed from McGuire AFB in New Jersey, arrived at RAF Mildenhall and then took a bus to his or her assigned base. While I was waiting in the airport terminal at

An evening at home with the family in 1974, while stationed at Whiteman AFB, MO. Sharing the couch with me is my wife Ruby. I am holding my son, Brian, and daughter Patti is sitting on the floor.

McGuire AFB to board my plane to England, I noticed a black staff sergeant staring at me. I could tell he was a security policeman because he was wearing the new security police beret. I nodded to acknowledge his stare and continued reading my book. He must have known that I was a security police officer by the shield on my uniform pocket; I had not yet been issued a beret. When I went into the cafeteria and sat down, the staff sergeant asked to join me. He introduced himself as SSgt. Herb Jones. Then he said, "Sir, I sure hope that you are going to RAF Mildenhall."

"As a matter of fact, Sergeant Jones, I am."

"Sir, are you the new squadron commander?" he asked eagerly.

"Yes, I am," I replied.

"Sir, I was praying that you were going to RAF Mildenhall because that's where I'm going. I have never worked for a black commander before and I was hoping to get to work for you."

"Great, Sergeant Jones. Looking forward to working with you, too."

"See you on the other side of the pond, sir," he said and went back into the waiting area.

When I arrived at the terminal at RAF Mildenhall I couldn't find my sponsor, Major Goldsmith, whom I would be replacing. After waiting about forty-five minutes I left the terminal to look for him but there was no sign of him anywhere. A security police patrol car arrived and the driver asked, "Major Hoffler, can I give you a ride to your quarters?"

I was surprised. "How did you know my name?" I asked the driver, a black staff sergeant named David Ebo. Ebo said he was SSgt. Herb Jones' sponsor and that he had just picked him up. SSgt. Jones told Ebo that they had a new black squadron commander.

"I'm waiting for Major Goldsmith, have you seen him?" I asked Ebo.

"Yes, sir, he was here when the plane landed." Ebo broke out in laughter.

"What's the matter?" I asked.

Ebo got control of himself. "Sir, Major Goldsmith was here looking for you but he probably never considered that you might be black so, not seeing who he expected, he left."

"That's odd," I replied. "Shouldn't he have waited for all the majors to clear customs, rather than looking for a white major in a beret? After all, I have my security police shield on my uniform."

"Sir, you'll see a lot of surprises around here," Ebo confided. "When they see you, this squadron is going to go crazy. There aren't too many black majors in the security policeman career field and to be a commander too, some of these troops won't know how to act."

"Well, thanks for the information, Sergeant Ebo, but I think I can handle it."

"I am sure you can, sir," he replied.

What Ebo had said really surprised me. I was not naïve enough to think that all whites would readily accept me as their commander, or that all black airmen would work harder because their commander was black. But my philosophy was to see everyone as an individual and grade him or her as such.

When I met with Maj. Goldsmith the next day, he was surprised to see me. He asked me when I got in and I said that I had arrived on my flight as scheduled. He was very apologetic for not picking me up. Apparently what Ebo had said was correct. Maj. Goldsmith had been looking for a white security police officer and missed me. The following day I met my new commander, the base commander. After the usual introductions, the colonel told me that he hoped I would command the squadron as well as Maj. Goldsmith had. I assured him that I would. Later I learned that the squadron had received a "marginal" rating on its previous inspection. Yet the base commander was telling me that he hoped I would do as good a job as Maj. Goldsmith had done? In fact, I did much better. In my first two years at Mildenhall my squadron received the first "excellent" rating for a Security Police Squadron in the history of USAFE (United States Air Force-Europe). In 1978 my squadron was named the "Best Security Police Squadron" in USAFE and the best in the Air Force for 1978 overall.

CHAPTER 8

FIRST DAYS AT THE ACADEMY

In June 1979, I arrived at the United States Air Force Academy in Colorado Springs, Colorado, to my new assignment as the commander of the 7625th Security Police Squadron. At first I wondered why I had been chosen for this assignment. The United States Air Force Academy is a special assignment and normally one has to apply to be assigned there. I had never applied and, frankly, I was not even aware that the USAF Academy had a Security Police Squadron commander's position available at that time. In other words, my record of consistently high efficiency ratings earned me a prestigious assignment to the United States Air Force Academy.

Even with my impressive record supporting me, I still faced some hostility from members of my squadron. They perceived that I had been chosen for this prestigious position solely because I was black. Not only that, but my predecessor as squadron commander had been aware of the sensitive racial climate at the academy and had exploited that climate to my detriment. He said that I had been chosen because I was a black officer and he spread that information around the squadron, stirring up resentment and trouble before I even arrived. He positioned me as an "affirmative

73

action" selection. I'm not sure why he wanted to stir up this kind of trouble. Perhaps he was upset because he could not choose one of his friends to be his replacement.

My predecessor left the academy for his next assignment about two months before I arrived. In the interim, the operations officer had served as commander. This was his first assignment in the security police career field after spending some years as enlisted in another career field. That he resented having me as his commander became more and more obvious as time passed. His resentment was not based on my race. The captain was okay in that area. I felt that he resented my management style. I was too strict compared to his previous commander.

On my second day as squadron commander, the day shift flight chief, who was white, came into my office and said, "Major, has anyone given you a tour of the academy grounds yet?" It was something the operations officer should have volunteered to do.

"No."

"Major, I've got time, let's go for a ride," and he gave me a tour of the academy grounds in his patrol car. Our conversation during that ride began uneasily. "Sir, some of the whites do not like the fact that you are here," he said. "Some have never seen a black security police major or had a black commander before."

I bristled. "Sergeant, they should look at what is on my shoulder rather than the color of my skin."

"I know Major, but it isn't that way here. The colonel and the captain are afraid that you are going to upset their good thing." Although the colonel had moved on to another assignment, he still had a lot of buddies in the squadron.

The flight chief's words struck me like a cannonball. I could not understand why a colonel, the previous squadron commander, who had moved on to another assignment, would worry about what was happening in my squadron. I considered meddling in my squadron as very unprofessional.

"Thank you for the information, Sergeant," I replied evenly, "but as long as I have support up on the hill, I can handle myself." ('Up on the hill' referred to the command section of the academy.)

The next day, the operations officer accompanied me to my first staff meeting and introduced me to the staff. After the staff meeting, a black colonel, who was the chief of plans and programs, asked me to come by his office before I left the building. He was a very impressive man with a deep, sonorous voice. I could see by the wings on his uniform that he was a pilot. In my seventeen years in the Air Force, I could count the number of black pilots I had seen on both of my hands. He proceeded to tell me that he was also a lawyer and a graduate of Howard University in Washington, D.C. "Major, do you know how you received this assignment?"

"No, sir," I replied.

"Well, let me fill you in. Last year some of the black officers here met with the superintendent of the academy and expressed concern that there were not enough senior black officers and noncommissioned officers assigned here to serve as role models and mentors to the cadets and the enlisted personnel. These officers suggested that the superintendent should get personally involved to ensure that more black officers and senior NCOs received assignments here."

"Wow." I had never heard of an arrangement whereby black officers and senior NCOs were specially selected to receive assignments to an Air Force base. The colonel told me that he was stationed at the Pentagon and was told by a general to "get out to the academy" because the Air Force Academy needed black officers. He said that he had been directed by the superintendent to chair a committee to review the personnel files of black officers for possible assignment to the academy.

"Major Hoffler, I picked you for this assignment," he said. "So I want you to make me proud."

"Yes, sir," I replied. "You don't have to worry about me, sir."

The colonel became my mentor. Whenever I saw him, he would always ask how things were going. I would say, "Fine, sir" and things were truly fine.

One day I received a telephone call from the commander of the Civil Engineering Squadron, who arrived at the academy shortly after me. He was another black officer recruited for the academy and was considered a "fast burner." He was promoted below the zone to major, lieutenant colonel and colonel. He was also the finest example of a military officer I ever met: always professional, uniform creased and many ribbons. However, he was upset because the gate guards would not salute his wife when she drove through the gates at the academy. I tried to explain to him that gate guards do not salute the decal on the car, only the person in the car. When they recognize that the person in the vehicle is not an officer, they are not required to salute. "The gate guards know that your wife is not an officer," I explained. "So when you are not in the vehicle, they are not required to salute her."

Unfortunately, that explanation was not good enough for the colonel. He wanted the gate guard to salute his spouse because she was driving his vehicle, which had an officer's decal displayed. Whenever she drove through the gate, I would get a telephone call from the colonel chewing my butt for the gate guard not saluting her.

I was put into quite a dilemma. There was no way I was going to tell my gate guards to start saluting officers' decals regardless of who was driving but I could no longer take those butt chewings from the colonel; nor did I want to elevate the problem to our supervisor, the chief of staff. So I called my mentor, and explained the situation to him.

At first he laughed and said that sounds just like something the colonel would do. "Joe, I'll call him and your problem will be solved." I never received another telephone call from the colonel on that subject.

On the way back to the office, the captain asked me how I was going to "run" the squadron. "What do you mean?" I asked.

"Well, Ron used to let me do whatever I wanted," he explained as we drove across the academy grounds. "I usually work on special projects."

"Special projects?" I asked.

"Special projects like providing support for the many parades and social functions at the academy," he explained.

"By the way, Captain, who is Ron?" I inquired. I really did not know who "Ron" was.

"Colonel Peacock," he replied.

It never occurred to me that a junior officer would refer to his commander by his first name. "Pull off the road and stop the car," I ordered. He complied. "Captain, in my presence you will always refer to a senior officer by his rank and not by his first name."

I could see that he was very upset. Apparently "Ron," the previous squadron commander, had never spoken to him like that.

"Yes, sir," he muttered, shaking his head.

As I was walking through the front door of the building a few days later, an airman passed by me without saluting. When I asked him why he did not salute, he replied that the front of the building had been declared a "non-salute" area. That just did not sit right with me. I knew I was at the Air Force Academy. But a "no salute zone" needed further research on my part. Once I reached my office, I called in the operations officer and asked him who had designated the front of the building a "non-salute" area.

"I did," he replied.

I reached into my bookcase, opened the base regulations and read to him that only the chief of staff could designate a non-salute area. "I want the designation changed immediately," I said. "What would happen if the superintendent or the chief of staff visited the building? An airman could walk past him without saluting. You have taken it upon yourself to authorize an airman to not salute a general or colonel? That is unbelievable."

There was more to being a security policeman than simply providing support for parades and social functions but it was obvious to me that the captain had been given free rein by my predecessor to do as he pleased.

The series of unpleasant surprises continued during my first months at the academy. One day, I asked the operations officer if I could see the duty officer reports. He told me that there weren't any.

"You mean to tell me that there isn't a duty officer scheduled to make after-duty-hour visits to the flight personnel?" I was astonished.

"No, sir," he replied. "The colonel never installed that kind of program."

I instructed the captain to create a duty officer roster made up of all E-7s and above. "They will pull duty officer for a week at a time and make at least two after-duty-hour post checks and prepare a written report to me on their findings," I said. An after-hour post check by senior security police personnel is essential to troop morale and discipline. I had never heard of a Security Police Squadron that did not require after-duty-hour post checks by senior personnel.

The lack of discipline and consistency in the Security Police Squadron on the academy continued to astound me. One day as I watched guard mount, the formation that security policeman form prior to going on duty, during which their uniforms are inspected and they receive the instructions for that shift, I noticed that some squadron members wore short-sleeved shirts and some long-sleeve shirts.

After the flight broke formation, I approached the captain about the non-conformity of the uniforms and explained that such variety was unacceptable. I did not really care if everyone wore short sleeves or long sleeves; I only cared that they were consistent. With the exception of the gate guards, the whole flight should dress alike. I was not singling out the captain for criticism. I was trying to bring some professionalism to a security police squadron that was being operated by a young captain with no prior security police experience, and a previous commander who was more of a politician than a true security police officer.

My motivation to instill some professionalism into the unit was my own personal high performance standards. A letter in the commander's file dated May 1978 from the commandant of cadets, a brigadier general, confirmed my initial assessment of the squadron's leadership. The letter addressed to the commander stated in part:

> *Shortly after my arrival at the academy, I called you personally regarding the lack of military courtesy demonstrated by the security police manning our gates. Since that time I have noted very*

little, if any, improvement. I find the courtesy and service being provided totally inconsistent with the high standards of job performance we must have here at the Air Force Academy.

In July 1980, I received a call from my supervisor, the chief of staff, Colonel Gordon. Col. Gordon supported my attempts to instill some professionalism into the squadron. He asked if I was having any difficulty with the captain and I replied, "Yes, somewhat. He had obviously been given free rein by the previous squadron commander. He's great at handling special events at the academy, but he lacks basic security police skills. Overall, he is really an outstanding officer. I wish I had him before he was exposed to the previous squadron commander."

"Would you have any problems with him transferring to the plans and programs section at the academy?" he asked.

"No," I replied. "I think that would be a great move for him and for the squadron because he is not directing them in any basic security police skills at the moment."

The chief of staff agreed to approve the transfer now that he knew how I felt about it. I expressed my appreciation for his asking my opinion and dismissed myself from his office.

Back at my office, it became apparent what had happened. When I arrived there, the captain was waiting to see me. Evidently, he had gone around me to his "friends" in the plans and programs section and requested a transfer. He asked if I had spoken to the chief of staff. I told him that I had, and that I had approved his transfer. I wished him luck in his new assignment and asked why he was leaving the unit.

"I don't want to work for you," he replied, not looking me in the eye.

"Why not?" I asked. "It's okay, you can speak freely."

He took a deep breath. "Because you are too strict for me," he answered. "Since you've come from Europe you haven't adjusted to the way the USAF Academy does things. Sir, you act like you are fighting a war in Europe. This is the Air Force Academy." His comments caught me off-guard but I retained my composure.

I said, "Captain, police work is police work. I have been in the security police field for more than sixteen years. The academy is a unique assignment and all you are doing is coordinating special events. Unless you have your troops following Air Force regulations, they will be lost when they get to a real Air Force base. There is more to policing than football games, and crowd and traffic control for cadets' social events," I explained, then dismissed him from my office.

Even as I worked my squadron into shape, I learned more and more about how lax things had been under my predecessor. One of the NCOs in charge of the training section owned a hot tub franchise in town and was using the training section's second telephone number as his business number. One day I called the seldom-used telephone number for the security police training section and, sure enough, someone answered, "Green Springs Hot Tub." I told him that I did not want him using a government telephone line as his own commercial number. Then I asked him to come to my office immediately. When he reported to me, he apologized and promised that he would not use that number again for his business. "I should hope not," I replied.

About eighteen months into my assignment at the Air Force Academy, in the summer of 1981, the senior NCO, a senior master sergeant, was due to transfer. I saw an opportunity to upgrade the position by requesting that HQ Air Force assign a chief master sergeant to the unit. A chief is the highest enlisted rank in the Air Force and carries a lot of prestige within the service. A chief could help the squadron improve the number of airmen selected for Airman of the Quarter, Airman of the Year, and other similar honors.

HQ Air Force searched the Air Force for a chief master sergeant to receive the prestigious assignment to the USAF Academy. Meanwhile at a base south of Colorado Springs, the chief in the Security Police Squadron was due for reassignment. To save on relocation costs, the personnel people asked if I would consider accepting a chief master sergeant who was stationed locally for my new position.

On paper, the chief seemed perfect for the position. He had a college degree; and having previously worked in the cadet area, he knew the important relationship between the cadets and the enlisted personnel on the base. I called his commander and asked for his assessment of the chief. The commander gave him high marks. When I met the chief for a personal interview, I was very impressed. He was sharp and articulate. Being prior enlisted myself, I had always had a deep respect for NCOs and especially for chiefs. I explained to him that I wanted a chief to serve as a role model for the squadron's enlisted personnel, to become involved in the chief's group at the academy and to better assist the enlisted personnel in all areas. I said that by the unit not having a chief, we were losing out in some areas of personnel improvement. I told him that he would also be the acting first sergeant and personnel person. I found it unbelievable that a Security Police Squadron did not have a full-time first sergeant prior to that, but my predecessor obviously hadn't thought it important. The chief accepted my conditions of assignment and assured me that he would fulfill my expectations.

The academy had recently been assigned a new superintendent, who was hard but fair. I liked working for him, and he clearly liked his security policemen, perhaps because we had made such a good first impression on him.

When the new superintendent made his first visit to the academy, he arrived at the north gate at around 0300 hours. Since the north gate is the less-traveled gate, the gate guard is more likely to be dozing off at that time of night. However, when he when drove up to the gate, the guard was awake and very alert. He gave the superintendent a sharp salute and precise directions to his quarters. From that point on, the Security Police Squadron could do no wrong in the superintendent's eyes. That speaks volumes for good first impressions.

The new superintendent had instituted a policy that no one from another base in the Colorado Springs area could transfer to the academy without his personal approval. This meant that if I wanted the chief, I had to request permission from the superintendent. So I first met with my supervisor, the chief of staff, and explained why I thought that having a chief in the squadron would be a morale booster for the enlisted personnel.

"Joe, I agree with you," he said. "The Security Police Squadron needs a chief. But we have to convince the 'old man' and you know his policy; he wants to prevent people from 'homesteading' in the Colorado Springs area. There are some people who go from Peterson AFB to Cheyenne Mountain AFB to the academy and spend their whole careers in this area."

"Yes, sir. I understand. But I have interviewed the chief and I think he will be a great fit for the squadron."

Later, when the chief of staff and I met with the superintendent, I explained the benefits to the enlisted men and women of the unit of having a chief. I also said that I had interviewed the chief and found him to be a great fit for the unit. The superintendent approved our request. As we left his office, he said, "Joe, you guys are doing a great job down there so keep up the good work. If you need anything else, let me know."

"Yes, sir," I replied proudly.

Having filled the requirement for a chief, my next major task to improve the squadron was to get a full-time first sergeant assigned. Although the first sergeant's duties were being filled by the chief on a part-time basis, security police duties are so demanding that every security police unit needs a full-time first sergeant to deal with the personnel problems that come up every day, so I asked the chief to find me one. I reviewed some files and recommended a master sergeant to be the squadron's first sergeant This proved to be a really great move. He had been a security policeman himself and understood the typical problems and concerns of security policemen. Slowly but surely I felt that things were falling into place and I was creating a first-class squadron that the Air Force Academy and I could be proud of. I had recruited a new operations officer with previous security police experience and received approval for two new positions for the squadron: a chief master sergeant and a first sergeant. Although I was falsely accused of only recruiting blacks, it should be noted that all of the above were white. If only I had known then how all my hard work and effort would be rewarded later on.

CHAPTER 9

SQUADRON DEEMED TOO BLACK

One day I received a call from SSgt. Ravenell. Johnnie had worked for me as an airman back in 1969 at RAF Greenham Common in England, where I was his first officer supervisor. He had heard from a technical sergeant, who worked for me at RAF Mildenhall, that I was now assigned to the USAF Academy and he called to say how much he enjoyed working for me and how much I had helped shape his career. It always felt good to hear that from an airman whom I knew when he first joined the Air Force. Ssgt. Ravenell asked if I had any open positions for him at the academy. After checking the personnel roster and his performance reports I requested that he join us at the academy. The day shift flight chief is senior in rank to the other flight NCOs, which meant that by tradition, he would be the flight chief for the day shift, which was one of the prime positions. I really had no idea of Ravenell's time-in-grade before I brought him on board. My sole concern was bringing another outstanding NCO to the squadron.

MSgt. Walker, another black NCO who had served with me in England, also called and asked if I had a slot for him. I checked with the chief and we had a vacancy for a master sergeant to replace the person who managed security operations and was leaving for Europe. So at my request, the chief processed the paperwork to bring him to the academy. He was very sharp in appearance and very demanding of the troops. After his arrival, another master sergeant, who is also black, arrived at the academy, followed by two administrative personnel, both of whom are black.

I did not know either of them prior to their assignments to the USAF Academy. The staff sergeant ran the orderly room and the sergeant was assigned to work in the report and analysis section.

It is important to mention that white personnel were coming into the squadron as well during this period but seeing so many blacks being assigned to the Security Police Squadron in such a short period of time apparently caused concern among some white members. In hindsight, it appears that the arrival of two senior black NCOs was the impetus for the chief to begin his campaign of racial backstabbing against me.

My new operations officer arrived in the summer of 1983 and brought a breath of fresh air to the squadron. The captain is an Italian-American from New York. Unlike my previous operations officer, he had spent six years in the security police career field at an Air Force base in the northeastern part of the United States and was well versed in security police work and traditions. The captain was hardworking and conscientious. He and I really hit it off. However, some of the enlisted members of the squadron didn't like him because he wasn't as lax with them as the previous captain had been.

Not long after his arrival, the chief called him into his office one day and asked him to close the door behind him. "Captain, have you noticed what is going on around the squadron?" Chief Michaels asked.

"No," the captain replied. "What do you mean?"

"I've talked with some of the troops and they feel that blacks are taking over the unit and that we must do something about it."

Operations officer and I at a surprise birthday party the squadron gave me in 1983.

"What are you implying?" he asked. "Blacks are taking over? Taking over what? This is the United States Air Force."

"There is a black commander, a black day flight commander, a black NCOIC of operations, a black NCOIC of the orderly room and a black NCOIC of investigations," he responded.

The operations officer was adamant. "Chief, I don't want to hear that kind of talk from you again," he said. "The next time I do, I am telling the colonel. You can share with him your racial hang-ups. He expects you to improve relations among the younger troops, not tear them apart."

Unfortunately, he didn't tell me about this conversation with the chief until much later. If only he had told me sooner, perhaps I could have been prepared for the firestorm of racism and prejudice that was heading my way.

In December 1983, I received a call from my career advisor at Headquarters Air Force Personnel Center telling me that I was "looking good" for promotion to colonel. However, he said that he wanted me to extend my tour at the academy for three or four months beyond my scheduled departure date of June 1984 until the promotion board met in September or October. If I left at my scheduled departure date in June it would make it difficult for him to reassign me. He explained that without a promotion, he could not assign me to a full colonel's slot. On the other hand, if he were to assign me to a lieutenant colonel's slot and I got promoted, he would have to reassign me again shortly thereafter.

He said that it would be best for all concerned if I extended my tour at the academy. I really did not anticipate any problems with getting an extension so I said, "Okay, I'll talk to the chief of staff, Colonel Weaver."

The next day I went to see my supervisor, the chief of staff, Col. Weaver, but he was on vacation so I spoke with the deputy chief of staff. I explained the situation to the deputy chief of staff and to my surprise he said he would not approve me for an extension. Shocked, I asked why. His feeble reply was that I had been at the academy too long already and he thought it best if I moved in June as planned or retired.

"Some people have been at the academy for ten years," I countered. "Why are you giving me that reason?"

"That's my decision," he replied.

"When will Colonel Weaver return?" I asked.

"Monday."

"Fine. I will speak with him then," I said, maintaining my composure as I saluted and excused myself from his office.

On the drive back to my office, I sensed that something was amiss. Why would the deputy chief of staff deny my request for an extension based on me being at the academy too long? He arrived at the academy a few months after me. It was okay for him to stay longer, but not me. When I reached my office I called in the captain and told him about my conversation with the deputy chief of staff. He also seemed puzzled that the deputy chief of staff would deny me an extension, or at least make it very difficult for me to extend my tour.

"Don't worry about it, Colonel H.," he counseled. "Just enjoy your weekend. I'm sure that Col. Weaver will approve your extension."

The following Monday I reported to Colonel Weaver as planned. He said that if he were going to stay at the academy, he would approve my extension. I had done an outstanding job and deserved a level opportunity at the promotion board. Then he dropped a bombshell.

"However, Marty is going to be the new chief of staff after I leave and he will not approve your extension," Col. Weaver added.

I was flabbergasted. "Colonel, may I have your permission to see the superintendent?" I asked.

"That won't do any good," he said. "Marty expected you to respond this way so he has already briefed the superintendent, who will support his decision."

My mind was racing. "Sir, may I extend until September 30, since that will give me twenty-two years of service? Also, the promotion board may meet in September."

"Yes. And good luck on the board."

I thanked Col. Weaver for his time, saluted, and dismissed myself from his office. If only I had known then what I would later find out. Deputy Chief of Staff Smith knew that he would become chief of staff, and therefore my supervisor, on March 11, 1984. So he timed his "smear" campaign to coincide perfectly with the change in leadership at the academy.

Some background on the new chief of staff may be helpful here. In my opinion, he was virulently racist against black Air Force officers.

For some reason, he did not treat black enlisted personnel with the same scorn that he reserved for black officers. I spoke to black enlisted personnel who worked for him and they thought he was just great. For some reason, he did not think blacks should be officers in the Air Force and if so, definitely not assigned to the USAF Academy. To the new chief of staff, blacks were not qualified to command. When I thought about my meeting with Col. Weaver, a cold chill came over me. I knew at that point that my whole career might be in jeopardy. Without the chief of staff's support, I could be in serious trouble for promotion.

On the surface the new chief of staff's lack of support did not make sense to me. I wondered why a new manager would want to replace a commander like me, with five years of experience on the job, with a new commander with no experience at the academy. The only possible answer was that he simply did not want a black commander working under him. With his contacts at HQ Air Force Personnel, he could raise the question of race with his friends and be assured that my replacement would be white. My perception of Chief of Staff Smith was developed by his treatment of black officers who worked for him, encouraging them to curtail their tours. It seemed that he did all he could to rid the academy of black officers, performing his own version of "ethnic cleansing." When informed, the USAF did nothing to stop him. If I had rotated from the academy in June 1984, as the new chief of staff wanted me to, he would have been my supervisor from March 11 to June 30 of that year.

I had to try to circumvent his racist actions because I definitely did not want him to write an officer effective report (OER) on me that would be on the top of my personnel file at the promotion board.

I had discussions with my career advisor at the HQ Personnel Center and the NCOIC of the OER section at the academy about how to prevent the chief of staff from writing an OER on me. Their conclusion was if I submitted my retirement paperwork to retire in September, he would not have the chance. I could then meet the promotion board in September, when I was still on active duty, and with Col. Weaver's outstanding OER on top. Once I submitted my retirement paperwork, all performance reports on me would stop.

Submitting my retirement paperwork was a sad action for me. At the time, I felt that I had no other choice. I had to do something to circumvent the racist actions of the new chief of staff and give myself an opportunity at being promoted. At this point, I did not have any hard evidence that Chief of Staff Smith was a racist; I was just acting on my "gut." Frankly, I thought I had defeated him. However, I had no idea how deeply ingrained racism was in him and that he would take such illegal and unethical actions to stop me. Up until that point, I had been a thirty-year man, "gung ho" all the way and bleeding Air Force blue. The Air Force had been very good to me and I had been very good to it in return. I had never considered retiring before having the chance to get promoted to colonel. I had worked so hard and so long for that opportunity and I was so close...until the new chief of staff got in my way.

During my assignment at the academy, I had received all outstanding performance reports with generals' endorsements; I had completed all of my professional military education, I had earned an MBA in 1976 and I was in a promotable position. My predecessor was promoted to colonel. (Also my successor was promoted to colonel while in this position.)

When I returned from the personnel office, I told the captain that I planned to submit my retirement paperwork to prevent the new chief of staff from writing a negative performance report on me.

"Why are you doing this, Colonel H.?" he asked. "The new chief of staff can't be that bad."

"Captain, I tell you, there is something about him and black officers. If he were fair, he would have let me extend my service through the colonel's selection board."

"Yeah, Colonel H., you do have a point there," he said.

I told Ruby of my sudden plan to submit my retirement paperwork. She was puzzled and wondered why I had to do all of this just to avoid the new chief of staff writing a report on me. "This guy doesn't even know you," she argued. "You haven't worked for him for one day. How do you know he will give you a bad OER? You have never had one. Why would you get one now?"

"Dear, there is something about his past actions with black officers," I explained. "It's like he believes that people of African descent are cursed from birth or something and not qualified to be leaders. So how can I expect him to treat me fairly?"

All of my actions were to no avail. The new chief of staff, having spent many years in the personnel career field, seemed to sense what I was doing. Once my retirement was approved, he could not write a performance report on me, meaning that I could meet the colonel's promotion board with the outstanding OER that I had received from Col. Weaver on top of my file, and most likely get promoted. But he could not allow that to happen. He had to devise something to put a negative report into my personnel file.

After my conversation with the then deputy chief of staff in which he suggested that I retire or move on, I had some sense of the plot brewing against me, but it would be a long time before I was aware of all of the sordid details. So many things were happening that I knew nothing about. A1C Stover, whom I mentioned earlier (in Chapter 1), had already taken up his sinister role in the plot against me.

A1C Stover was a white airman with discipline and performance problems. He was twenty-two years old, compared to the average age of eighteen or nineteen, so he tried to create a more mature image of himself. He always presented what he considered to be a Marine's appearance: His uniform was always neatly pressed and he tried to talk like an ex-Marine. He always addressed senior personnel with a stern, "Yes, sir." However, when he wasn't trying to impress senior personnel in the squadron that he was a top performer, his voice and attitude would change. His coworkers and immediate supervisors, who worked with him every day, knew the real Stover.

In addition to his discipline and performance problems, the "real" Stover had a history of lying and deception. For example, he told his supervisor and others in the unit that he was a prior Marine, which he wasn't.

In February 1984, I received a visit from two Teller County sheriff's deputies, who had formerly been assigned to the academy's Security Police Squadron. They informed me that they had heard that A1C Stover was bragging about harming several people over a broken love affair. That information was serious, given the fact that security policemen are armed. So I called in the captain and the first sergeant and briefed them on what I had heard. We three agreed that before Stover harmed himself or someone else, it was best to follow established security police procedures and have him evaluated by the mental health department at the academy hospital. So I removed A1C Stover's authority to carry a weapon and the first sergeant made an appointment for him with a therapist at the hospital.

Following established security police procedures, until Airman Stover could see the social worker, he was assigned duties around the squadron that did not require him to be armed. A security police commander cannot allow a service member to be issued a weapon once it is known that he has personal problems, until a therapist sees him. We had been following that procedure for a combined total of forty years at many Air Force installations.

A1C Stover was not singled out for any excessive vindictive treatment as alleged by the academy's chief of staff and the academy inspector general's investigating officer. He was assigned to the vehicle section to assist the squadron's supply NCOIC.

Of special note here is the date and subject of Stover's original complaint to the academy's inspector general. Following what was normally a temporary personnel action, Stover decided to get revenge. On February 6, Stover made a complaint centering on what he viewed as fraud, waste and abuse in the Security Police Squadron, happenings that he claimed to have witnessed while he was working on his detail in the vehicle section and at a party on base at a sergeant's house. The sergeant was the subject of the complaint; I was not mentioned. Also, on February 6, 1984, my supervisor was still Col. Weaver, who had always treated me fairly and with respect. The academy inspector general waited more than thirty days to begin questioning the Security Police Squadron about Stover's complaint after the deputy chief of staff assumed the position of chief of staff. They also recruited A1C Stover to "dig up dirt" on me and ignored his original complaint as it did not contain charges against me. Then they could choose their investigator, the cadet group commander, and get the result they wanted. This is exactly what they did. They violated the academy's regulation that required the USAF Academy inspector general to choose the next officer on a roster to be the investigator. The roster was kept in the academy's personnel section.

As with everything in this case, Air Force and academy rules and regulations did not apply to the chief of staff and inspector general. The selection of the cadet group commander is interesting for another reason. He was not a disinterested party as required in this investigation. He and I were meeting the same selection board for promotion to colonel. Therefore, he had an interest in ensuring that something negative was inserted into my personnel file. As such, he was not able to be sufficiently disinterested in the outcome of the investigation. According to Air Force regulations, an investigating officer must be impartial, unbiased, objective, and thorough. The appointment of the investigating officer was contrary to regulations.

In late February 1984, the captain and the first sergeant reported that some of the airmen in the squadron were complaining that A1C Stover was trying to get them to make statements about the commander. Stover claimed to be on a special mission for the inspector general of the academy to gather dirt on the commander. As unbelievable as it may seem now, that part of his story was true. Here was an airman who had been in the Air Force for less than a year and was a non-performer, yet he was recruited by the inspector general of the Air Force Academy to interview the airmen in the squadron to gather dirt on the commander. The captain told me that he had spoken to Stover, who confirmed that the USAF Academy inspector general asked him to dig up some dirt on me for the new chief of staff.

In response to complaints by members of the squadron that A1C Stover was bugging them for "dirt on the commander," the captain told them to ignore Stover and not get involved. But the information gathering continued and eventually, at the request of the first sergeant, I brought Stover into my office and questioned him about his actions.

A1C Stover insisted that the inspector general had asked him to gather negative information about me. This seemed too incredible to be true, so I chewed him out about lowering morale in the unit. "If I hear about you asking questions about me again, I will see your damn ass out of the front gate," I warned him and then dismissed him. I later learned that after our conversation, A1C Stover reported to the IG that personnel in the squadron were harassing and threatening him so that he could not do his job of gathering dirt on the commander.

A1C Stover's only friends in the unit were two young airmen. Both were troubled men with axes to grind within the squadron. One airman's duty performance was below par and he was close to being discharged. In fact, a few months prior to this, a discharge package had been prepared for him but I decided to give him another chance to prove himself in the Air Force. A1C Stover's other friend had been known to brag around the unit that he and the chief of staff were good friends who belonged to the same church. He told many of the other airmen that if they had any problems in the squadron to tell him. He would inform the chief of staff, and the more information the better, because the chief of staff wanted to get rid of Lt. Col. Hoffler.

This brings me back to the beginning of my story. The new chief of staff, as I mentioned, assumed the position on March 11, and officially became my supervisor. My brother John had been diagnosed with cancer prior to that, so I was planning to be away visiting him in Maryland. The new chief of staff knew exactly when I would be gone.

The day before I left for Maryland, on March 20, I had my fateful meeting with the academy's inspector general's investigating officer in which he asked me all those suspicious questions about gambling with airmen and taking that piece of scrap Plexiglas. Because he did not "read me my rights" or take notes during our conversation and was not authorized to investigate fraud, waste and abuse items, I considered my session with him just an informal discussion. He did not give me any indication that he was going to question any of the airmen in my squadron. I was under the impression that the discussion ended with that conversation. It is obvious that he framed our meeting to look like a talk between two lieutenant colonels. With me being a security policeman, he knew I was well aware of the Article 31 rights under the UMCJ; and if properly notified that I was a subject of an investigation involving theft of government property, I would have rightly exercised my Constitutional rights and requested an attorney.

I left for Maryland the next day. While at my brother's house, I received the frantic phone call from the captain informing me about the investigation. When I got back to the academy, my office was full of personnel wanting to report the harsh treatment they received from the academy's investigating officer, including cursing and yelling at them to give the "right" answers.

At that point I still believed that the new chief of staff would be a fair Air Force officer who would stop the investigating officer when he heard what was going on. But when I met with him upon my return to the academy, he became angry and accused me and other members of the squadron of interfering with an investigation. Obviously things were not going as well as he and the IG planned. No one in the squadron was properly informed that an investigation was ongoing. He threatened us with disciplinary action if we continued.

The captain, the first sergeant and I determined that the academy's chief of staff and the USAF Academy's inspector general were just using A1C Stover as a cover story. The real person behind the investigation was my own chief, Chief Michaels.

"Sir, remember when the chief told me that there were too many blacks in the squadron? Well, this must be his way of eliminating them, starting with you."

Oh, how I hoped that he was wrong, but every shred of evidence suggested that he was correct.

CHAPTER 10

A WITCH HUNT
IS LAUNCHED

I later found out that during this time period, the academy inspector general called the captain to his office and warned him to stay out of this situation. "They only want to get Joe," he was told.

"Who are they, and why are they after Lieutenant Colonel Hoffler?" the captain asked.

"It's none of your business," the inspector general replied curtly. "Just do as you are told and stop supporting Hoffler. This thing is bigger than you are, Captain."

The captain, however, being the loyal and conscientious person that he is, continued seeking the truth. He called two airmen into his office and advised them to ignore A1C Stover because the idea of airmen digging up dirt on a commander was beyond his comprehension.

The airmen refused to make incriminating statements against me to Stover, telling him they did not want to make a statement and that the captain had told them just to stay out of it. A1C Stover obviously had a direct line to the chief of staff because that information got back to him and he called the captain into his office to chew him out.

"Captain, you ignored the academy inspector general's recommendation to stay out of this. I urge you not to ignore my advice as well."

"Sir, I don't understand," the captain countered. "I am not doing anything. The squadron is in an uproar about this investigation and airmen are complaining to me about the academy's investigating officer and A1C Stover. What am I supposed to do?"

"Just stay out of it," the chief of staff repeated. "I know what I am doing. If I get word that you are talking to any of the airmen in that squadron I will cite you for interfering with an official investigation."

"Sir, this is not an investigation; this is a witch hunt," he argued. "Lieutenant Colonel Hoffler is a very good commander and you are listening to the bad apples in the squadron."

"Captain, I am warning you to butt out or I'll give you a letter of reprimand and ruin your Air Force career. I can't believe that you are falling on your sword for that..." He paused. "Captain, you are dismissed."

In April, a few weeks after the investigation began, the first sergeant informed me that the airman who babysat for the chief of staff's children and was his fellow church member was spreading a rumor around the squadron that Lt. Col. Hoffler was going to receive a letter of reprimand.

"I haven't heard anything from the chief of staff," I replied. I still had faith in the system, that Chief of Staff Smith would evaluate the facts and consider the biases of the sources. Then later that day the first sergeant heard at the academy bowling alley that I would be receiving a letter of reprimand from the chief of staff via base distribution, which represented the ultimate insult.

It was inconceivable that the chief of staff would leak out word of my punishment without discussing the findings with me first, and second, send a letter of reprimand via base distribution. This alone convinced me that he was more concerned with humiliating me than with disciplining me.

The next day, the captain brought a distribution envelope to my office. We sat there together and wondered before we opened it if the chief of staff would really be so low and unprofessional as to send a letter of reprimand via base distribution rather than call me into his office and discuss the disciplinary action privately. Slowly I opened the envelope and, sure enough, it was a letter of reprimand from the chief of staff. I had been in the Air Force for more than twenty-one years and had never seen anything like that, nor had anyone else in the room. *The chief of staff can only be a despicable racist and I am going to do everything in my power to stop him,* I told myself. I decided not to sign the letter and instead put it in my desk drawer. As difficult as it was emotionally, I resumed my official duties as squadron commander and acted as if nothing were wrong. Thank God I had the support of my senior NCOs and the captain, the squadron operations officer, who understood that I had been targeted solely because I am black. The captain had only been a member of the squadron for approximately ten months at that point, yet he was willing to put his military career on the line to help me.

After the next chief of staff's staff meeting, he called me into his office for a very tense meeting. "I want you to leave the squadron ASAP," he informed me. "I will grant you all the terminal leave you want."

"I do not want any terminal leave," I said evenly. "I am planning to stay on as commander until I retire, as Colonel Weaver and I agreed earlier."

"Have you received the letter of reprimand?" he asked.

"Yes," I replied sternly.

"Well, I have not received it back yet."

"I am not going to sign that letter because I did nothing to deserve it."

He leaned across his desk. "You will sign it."

"Sir, I will not. And I am not going to take terminal leave, either." I looked him straight in the eyes. "I came into this man's Air Force with my head held high and that is how I am leaving it."

"You will sign the letter of reprimand or I will give your captain one, too. As you know, that would ruin any chance he has of being promoted to major. Lieutenant Colonel Hoffler, I will relieve you of your duty as commander today," he threatened.

"On what grounds, sir?"

"I don't need any grounds," he answered. "My word is enough in the academy."

"Do as you please, sir," I said. "That is your decision, but understand that I am going to fight you all the way." Then I turned and walked out of his office.

When I returned to my office I called in the captain and told him what the chief of staff had said, including the threat to the captain's career. As I expected, he told me not to sign the letter of reprimand. "Colonel H., you did nothing wrong," he insisted. "You can't give in to him."

I appreciated the support but I had my doubts. "Captain, you don't understand. I'm sure that he's serious. He will destroy your career just as he's destroying mine. People like the chief of staff are mean racists. I have lived with his type all my life and if there is anything that a racist hates more than a black person, it is a white person who supports black people. The chief of staff, in my opinion, is worse than the KKK. At least the KKK wears white sheets, so you know who they are and what they stand for. He hides behind his blue United States Air Force uniform and does his dirty work in secret. He is a coward."

Throughout this whole ordeal, the chief of staff continued to routinely hold weekly staff meetings. After receiving the letter of reprimand in April, I found it extremely difficult to attend them. I always felt unwelcome by the chief of staff because I was black. He normally stared at me without acknowledging that I was a commander and an Air Force officer. Many times I considered sending my operations officer to the staff meeting in my place, but then I realized that that was exactly what the chief of staff wanted, to prevent me, the only black on his staff, from attending. I knew that he wanted to have an all-white staff meeting and I didn't want to nor could I be a part of letting that happen.

One day I had just had it with the chief of staff's insults and decided not to go to the meeting. I called the captain into my office and told him to go in my place. But then as he asked me why, my mind flashed back to other times and places where I had not been wanted either, such as the Woolworth's lunch counter sit-ins in Durham in the 1960s. "Captain, my family has been fighting discrimination since the Civil War," I explained. "See, the Confederate soldiers did not want my great-grandfather in the Union Army, just like the chief of staff does not want me in this Air Force. Nothing much has changed." After thinking back to my great-grandfather, I changed my mind, grabbed my coat and hat and went to the meeting. I was determined to prevent the chief of staff from having his all-white staff meetings as long as possible.

CHAPTER 11

ILLEGAL ACTIONS BY THE CHIEF OF STAFF

After much soul-searching and under duress to protect my operations officer, I decided to sign the letter of reprimand and returned it to the chief of staff just the way I received it, via base distribution. I continued to do my job as usual but about a week later, at the end of April, I received a telephone call from the officer who had been chosen to replace me as squadron commander. I knew him from the time we spent serving together in Thailand and when he was the security police commander at Lowery AFB near Denver.

"Joe, what is going on in the squadron?" he asked.

"What do you mean?"

"I got a call from the chief of staff telling me to get to the academy ASAP because the squadron was going downhill fast," he explained, sounding perplexed. "When are you retiring?"

I told him in September.

"Okay, I'll try to stall the chief of staff by telling him that I need time to sell my house in Florida and get my kids out of school," he continued.

"Look Joe, I don't want to do this to you. What kind of boss is he, anyway?"

"Well, you won't have any problems with him," I replied. "You're white."

"What do you mean?"

"The chief of staff is a racist and he's out to get me, simply because I am black."

He sounded shocked. "Okay," he said. "I'll stall here as long as I can. I know you don't want to just hang around and do nothing until you retire."

"You're right about that," I answered, then thanked him for his offer.

As I hung up the phone I understood that the chief of staff must have planned to relieve me of duty as soon as he could, whether I had signed the letter of reprimand or not. As I thought about the situation I couldn't help but hark back to an incident that had happened when I was at RAF Mildenhall in England, where I had a chance to see how racial incidents were meant to be handled, by professional military people.

When I was stationed at RAF Mildenhall in July 1977, the base commander, Colonel Merrill "Tony" McPeak, called me into his office one day. He said that he had a report from the base inspector general that a master sergeant, a member of my squadron, had made a complaint that because all of the security flight chiefs were black, I was a racist and had purposely placed blacks in senior roles. I was in shock. Flight chiefs are chosen by rank and placed into their positions by the security operations officer. I did not have anything to do with assigning the flight chiefs. To be candid, I wasn't even aware that all the security flight chiefs were black, which I explained to Col. McPeak. He understood and explained that he just wanted to get my side of the story. There was no inspector general investigation or any other actions taken in that case. How different that was from the case I now faced at the academy. Col. McPeak asked for and then listened to my side of the story, which was something the superintendent and chief of staff never did. Col. McPeak treated me like an officer, which was what I felt I

One of the awards I received on behalf of the squadron, 1977–78. Col. McPeak (left) attained the rank of 4-Star General and later became the chief of staff of the Air Force, the highest rank.

deserved after having served my country so admirably and for so long. He was subsequently promoted to general and named chief of staff of the USAF.

At the end of April, the first sergeant came into my office and told me that A1C Stover had been transferred out of the squadron. I was really angry. "Transferred by whom?" I asked.

He explained, "A1C Stover was bragging in the dormitory that the chief of staff transferred him to the Civil Engineering Squadron on the academy and then he will be going on to an Air Force base in Texas as a 'fully qualified security policeman.'"

This was another clear sign of the chief of staff undermining my authority as commander. I immediately called him, but he wasn't in so I then called the academy inspector general, and asked him who transferred one of my airmen without my authorization.

"The chief of staff did," he replied. "A1C Stover told him that he was being harassed by members of the squadron."

"That is not true," I responded. "No one in the squadron was harassing A1C Stover."

"The chief of staff is the chief of staff and he has the authority to transfer anyone he wants," the academy inspector general said angrily and then hung up the phone. The captain and the first sergeant heard the conversation. We looked at each other in total disbelief. How could an airman performing at such a low performance level have that much pull? "Can you believe that the chief of staff had the nerve to charge me with fraud, waste and abuse?" I asked them. "How much money do you think it cost the Air Force to transfer A1C Stover to another base?"

"Thousands, at least," the captain responded. "See, I don't think the chief of staff and inspector general expected Stover to openly question members of the squadron about 'digging up dirt on me' or to start bragging about his accomplishments. And once he did, that exposed their plan. His immaturity and narcissistic personality as diagnosed by the academy's social worker began to show, so they had to move him. They transferred him under the pretense that we, the squadron leaders, were harassing him. As you know, that was a bunch of bull. No one ever harassed Stover. The chief of staff made me so impotent as a squadron commander that I couldn't have harassed him if I'd wanted to."

"I wonder what travel code they used for Stover," the first sergeant asked. I responded, "Whatever he used was fraud and incorrect. I would love to see a copy of his travel orders."

"Look, first the chief of staff transferred A1C Stover to the Civil Engineering Squadron, without his commander or his first sergeant knowing about it," he continued. "Stover did not properly clear the squadron as required by Air Force regulations, which was illegal. Who signed his out processing paperwork in the first sergeant and commander's slots? "

"You're right, First Shirt," I replied. "The CE Squadron doesn't have a billet for a security policeman. Then from there, they transferred him to another Air Force base and reinstated him as a qualified security policeman. I have never heard of such a dirty deal, have you?"

"No, sir. Colonel H., this is unbelievable," the captain said. "A1C

Stover was obviously working for the IG and the chief of staff. Otherwise he would not have been shipped out like that. This is the 'smoking gun' in this whole dirty episode. It cost money to pay his travel and moving expenses. How can he get away with something like that?"

"Captain, have you ever heard the saying, 'Power corrupts and absolute power corrupts absolutely'?'"

"Yes, Colonel H., I have."

"Well, this is a prime example of such power."

"Where is the superintendent in all of this?"

"I wish I knew," I said.

He piped up again. "Sir, there is something else wrong here. A1C Stover has a 'seven' APR. A person can't transfer from the academy with a seven rating on his airmen performance report. The Air Force does not want to ship its 'bad apples' from one base to another." We three all looked at one another with the same ominous thought.

"You don't think the chief of staff and the academy inspector general changed Stover's performance report, do you?" the first sergeant asked.

"No, I don't think that even they would go that far," the captain argued.

"Captain, nothing seems beyond the chief of staff now," I replied.

"Do you think they would violate the sanctity of the Air Force's personnel records by tampering with them? For God's sake, the chief of staff was the director of personnel at the Air Force Academy for three years," the captain continued.

I shook my head. "First Shirt, this is your area, APRs. See what you can find out."

"Yes, sir. I'll get right on it."

After the first sergeant informed the captain and me that Airman Stover had been transferred to another base and made a fully qualified security policeman, the three of us, who, combined, had more than forty-five years of security police experience, became worried. The only way that Airman Stover could be re-qualified was by having his security police records cleansed. But cleansing his personnel record would deprive the new commander of pertinent information that he or she would need in order to make an evaluation of whether or not to issue A1C Stover a weapon. Obviously Stover's records had to have been cleansed because the Air Force wouldn't transfer an unqualified security policeman. I knew that the chief of staff was a dangerous person who would stop at nothing to carry out his policy of racism. However, this time, by cleaning out all of the negative information in Stover's records, he had possibly endangered the lives of personnel at A1C Stover's new base. At that point, until evaluated by a therapist and given the all clear, Stover should not have been issued a weapon.

During the summer of 1984, the captain and I mapped out our strategy to fight the racism and the total disregard for Air Force regulations by the academy's chief of staff and inspector general. While in my office discussing the options, the captain picked up the telephone and called the Headquarters Air Force inspector general office at Norton AFB, CA, and relayed what was going on at the USAF Academy. His actions even shocked me. I thought to myself, *I am the one being discriminated against and here is this white captain risking his military career by filing the complaint first. Unbelievable.* As soon as he mentioned the United States Air Force Academy, racism, possible tampering with military performance reports, and shady IG investigations, the duty officer did not want anything to do with the investigation.

"Refer this to your base inspector general," the duty officer advised.

"What?" he asked. "He's one of the guys who's in on the wrongdoings!"

We later discovered that personnel from the Headquarters Air Force inspector general called the academy inspector general office and reported that someone from the Security Police Squadron had called, trying to lodge a complaint, but that they refused to take it. So much for confidentiality when filing an inspector general's complaint against the Air Force Academy.

Later that summer, I attempted to enlist the help of two local civilian attorneys to help me "fight" my letter of reprimand from the chief of staff. But because it involved the Air Force Academy, one lawyer refused to take it. He told me that it would be a waste of his time and my money to go up against the Air Force Academy and that the Air Force protects the academy in all of its wrongdoings. I could not win. I left his office in disbelief after hearing that.

The other attorney wanted to take the case, however, he could not review it because I could not get a copy of the evidence against me. I kept the letter from the new academy inspector general, who was the investigating officer who had been promoted to the IG, denying my request to see the evidence against me.

Later, through the FOIO (Freedom of Information Office), I obtained a copy of the ruling by the academy legal office, confirming that my right to defend myself had been violated. I also contacted the academy's own legal office in April and requested their assistance in confronting the chief of staff. Because the legal office at the academy worked for the chief of staff, a major there referred me to the legal office at Lowery AFB in Denver. He scheduled a meeting for me at the academy with a captain. After explaining my case to him, including not being able to defend myself against the obviously erroneous investigation by the academy's investigating officer, the captain asked, "Why is the chief of staff giving you a letter of reprimand? You have twenty-two years of outstanding service, never even received a letter of counseling. I don't understand."

"Well, Captain, it is like this," I replied. "The only reason I can find is that I am black and the chief of staff is known for not liking black officers."

The captain assured me that he would do what he could to help. So I naturally asked how he was going to represent me if the academy would not allow him to see the "evidence" against me. He promised me that he would receive a copy of the report. However, as my attorney, the academy also refused him access to my report. He met with the chief of staff and then wrote him a letter detailing my accomplishments during my career and requesting that the letter of reprimand be rescinded. Unfortunately, the captain's efforts resulted in no action in my defense. The captain was handling numerous cases at the time and I suspect that he was spending only a minimum amount of time representing me when I needed this to be handled as the big-time case it was. The next day he called and said that the IG would not give him a copy of the investigation either. I've come to believe that the captain, my attorney, may have been threatened with career-altering actions if he helped me because suddenly he told me that that was all he could do. He refused to fight for me at all. To me this sounded like he expected me to "throw myself at the mercy of the court." I hated that approach, but at that point I wasn't in a position to reject suggestions from my legal officer. However, Law 101 provides information on protecting your client's rights, which obviously the captain, an attorney, was not aware of.

From April 9 through 12, the academy's Security Police Squadron hosted the security police Worldwide Symposium, which was a meeting of directors of security police from all the major commands in the Air Force. The superintendent of the academy welcomed the attendees to the symposium by praising my squadron and me for an outstanding job. Of course this was after my supervisor, the chief of staff, had given me the letter of reprimand and determined that I was doing a terrible job as commander. The symposium was a rousing success by all standards. The director of the security police career field, a brigadier general, was very complimentary of the job I had done hosting the event. On the afternoon of the final day of the symposium, he stopped by the office to say goodbye and to thank me personally and the squadron for a job well done.

While I had the brigadier general alone, I asked for his help in dealing with the chief of staff. I explained that he had personally prevented me from being promoted and was engaged in assassinating my character at every turn. I had known the brigadier general since my days as a commander in Europe, so I figured he could and would assist me. But instead he said, "Joe, I have known you for a long time and you have done an outstanding job here and at RAF Mildenhall. However, this is between you and the chief of staff."

"What?" I asked.

"Talk to him about it."

"But he won't even talk to me," I tried to explain. "The chief of staff refuses to hear my complaint."

"Joe, I can't help you. You must resolve this matter with the chief of staff," he said.

I was so angry and so disappointed that yet another person who had the power to help me wouldn't even take the time to listen to my concerns.

CHAPTER 12

PRESIDENT REAGAN'S VISIT TO THE USAF ACADEMY

Another high-profile event occurred in May 1984 when President Ronald Reagan spoke at the United States Air Force Academy's graduation ceremony. As was usual for a graduation ceremony in which the president of the United States was the guest speaker, the Secret Service was in charge of security, and the president's personal security was priority number-one. Following the attempt on President Reagan's life in 1981, his personal security had become even more important. The lead Secret Service agent and I developed a great rapport. He was from eastern North Carolina and had attended Albemarle College, which was next to my hometown.

Following what was the normal procedure when the president of the United States was the commencement speaker, I asked the surrounding military bases—Fort Carson, Peterson AFB, Cheyenne Mountain Complex, and Lowery AFB—along with the local civilian police agencies, including the Colorado Springs police, the El Paso County Sheriff's Department, and the Colorado Highway Patrol, to augment our security forces, which they all did. We also had assistance from the local FBI and Secret Service agents from Denver. You could say that we "maxed out" the law enforcement agencies within the local area.

The USAF Academy had a Plans and Program Division that was responsible for planning the other parts of the graduation. The division, for the first time, required graduation attendees to use tickets. As an additional measure to protect the president, for the first time, the Secret Service required that security walk-through metal detectors called "magnetometers" be placed at each gate into the football stadium where the graduation was being held. With President Reagan being such a popular president, we had the largest crowd ever for a graduation ceremony, exceeding all expectations. As this was the first time tickets were required for entry into the stadium, many people arrived without them and were therefore barred from entering. In addition, many of the metal detectors broke down and people were re-directed to gates where the security equipment worked. These two situations led to an extremely large and angry crowd gathering outside the stadium and in the parking lots.

Based on the potential threat of overcrowding and many people being outside of the stadium at the last minute, the Secret Service changed the original security plans and required us to secure the presidential convoy route from the Officers' Club to the stadium, a requirement that involved an additional twenty security personnel. In the initial plan, once President Reagan passed and entered the stadium, those additional troops would move to crowd control and then return to convey security prior to the president leaving the stadium. However, the Secret Service changed their plan and demanded that those troops stay in place to protect the convoy route during the president's speech, which limited the number of personnel available for crowd control. They told us that to provide increased security for the president, their security plans are always flexible.

During the graduation ceremony, I was positioned in the command post, with a view of the total area, with my controllers. The NCOIC security police operations and NCOIC plans and programs were at my side. Both were very knowledgeable of the procedures and had directed crowd and traffic control at two previous graduations. After President Reagan completed his speech it was a tradition for the United States Air Force Thunderbirds to fly over the stadium. As the president was completing his speech there came a frantic request from a major in the plans division. He had contacted the air traffic controllers and asked the NCOIC plans and programs, who was sitting in the security police command post, to move all of the people out of the area in and around the stadium parking lots or the Thunderbirds would not do their fly-over.

Both the NCOIC plans and programs and the NCOIC security police operations began frantically directing the remaining law enforcement troops, military and civilian, to move people out of the designated areas. However, the crowd was angry because they had missed seeing the president and the graduation ceremony and were now determined to get a close look at the Thunderbirds who would be flying directly overhead. For those reasons they refused to move. Ironically, it was the crowd itself that was preventing the Thunderbirds from flying. So the air traffic controllers refused to allow them to fly, which was embarrassing for the entire academy community. After the graduation ceremony, the special agent in charge stopped by my office and congratulated us on a job well done. "The president is leaving the academy unharmed and that is the only important item," he said, and as a token of his appreciation, he would send us mementos of President Reagan's visit.

The chief of staff, on the other hand, saw the graduation ceremony as another opportunity to embarrass and humiliate me personally. He placed the blame for the Thunderbirds not flying squarely on me. The academy held three meetings to critique the failure of the Thunderbirds fly-over and I wasn't invited to any of them. In fact, I was never asked by the superintendent or the chief of staff what had happened. Of course the chief of staff did not want to hear the truth. He was content both to disparage numerous civilian and military law enforcement agencies and to blame me for the Thunderbirds not performing on that day. As a military commander, I was acutely aware that I was required to take the blame when things went wrong on my watch. However, this was a situation in which nothing could have been done to move, in the time allowed, the many spectators who thought that they had the best seats for viewing the Thunderbirds flying over the stadium. In truth it was the chief of staff's own Plans and Program Division's lack of foresight and poor planning that led to the crowd overflow and the subsequent canceling of the fly-over. They failed to properly use the media to advertise that tickets would be required to enter the stadium to hear President Reagan. Therefore, many attendees, including family members, showed up without tickets and with Secret Service personnel staffing the gates, there were no exceptions for entry. Still, the chief of staff was not going to blame his own men when he could instead use the security police and me as his scapegoats.

(The Air Force congressional investigator, Col. Sung, followed the script of condemning anyone who filed a congressional complaint against the academy. However, during questioning by Col. Sung, my successor as security police commander stressed that after reviewing the plans for the stadium security, he was convinced that there was nothing the security police could have done differently and he thanked his God that he was not the security police commander that day because what happened was a series of bad events and no one person was to blame.)

A week after graduation, thank-you cards and cuff links arrived at the academy for key personnel in the Security Police Squadron from the Secret Service. NCOIC plans and programs and the captain received a set of presidential cuff links as gratitude for a job well done for protecting President Ronald Reagan during his visit to the USAF Academy. I did not receive anything so I called the Secret Service agent who told me that we would be receiving tokens of appreciation and asked if I was included in the list of "thank-you's." "Of course," the agent replied. My memento had been included along with the others. Just to be sure, I called the plans and programs section and the colonel in charge told me that a gift had arrived for me; however, the chief of staff did not think I was deserving so he denied it to me.

"So the chief of staff does not believe that President Reagan leaving the academy safely, without an attempt on his life, is important?" I asked.

The colonel had no reply.

After the graduation ceremony, word traveled around the academy and the local community that I was at fault for the Thunderbirds not flying that day. Many of my troops felt really bad about that news and came in to see me and apologize for what had happened. They knew that I wasn't personally responsible. To prove their point, one of the most treasured gifts I received at my retirement ceremony was a twenty-five by thirty-six-inch picture of the Thunderbirds flying over the United States Air Force Academy. Below the photo they had engraved, "Thanks and Good Luck from the LE Flight Personnel." Also, the captain offered to give me the presidential cuff links he received from the Secret Service for assistance during the cadets' graduation. Knowing that the chief of staff kept the set destined for me, initially, I refused them from the captain. He had earned them and I insisted that he keep them. However, I knew that he felt bad about how the chief of staff had blamed me personally for the mishap and that was his way of making it up to me. So I accepted the presidential cuff links and still have them today. I consider them one of my most treasured gifts from my twenty-two-year Air Force career.

CHAPTER 13

CHANGE OF COMMAND

As my days at the Air Force Academy wound down, everyone was surprised that the chief of staff ordered a change of command ceremony for when the new commander would take over my position. When you "fire" someone you don't normally order a change of command. I had mixed emotions about the event. On one hand I just wanted to ride off into the sunset, but on the other hand, I wanted to do the right thing by my troops, who had supported me throughout my ordeal.

It was a warm day that July when the first sergeant came into my office and told me that the chief of staff had directed him to plan a change of command ceremony.

"What?" I had asked, taken aback.

"Didn't you know, Colonel?"

"No," I replied. "And I don't want a change of command ceremony. The chief of staff has not discussed this with me." Normally the outgoing commander would request the ceremony. However, it had been over

121

four months since Chief of Staff Smith became the chief of staff and he and I had only had two conversations. One was when he asked me to retire and the second was when he threatened me with a letter of reprimand. In addition, I was suspicious about his motives. I wasn't scheduled to retire until September, so why was he pushing so hard for a change of command ceremony in July? The only conceivable answer was that he wanted to embarrass me by leaving me without a job for a few months, just hanging around the academy.

So the first sergeant went ahead and planned the ceremony, even as the chief of staff refused to discuss anything about it with me. A few days before the change of command ceremony, the new commander and his family arrived at the academy. In keeping with tradition, he stopped by to see the outgoing commander and the squadron. After discussing old times and his assignment at Homestead AFB in Florida, we got down to business. I told him about the unit, the unique aspects of policing at the Air Force Academy, and how this had been a great assignment for me up until the chief of staff took over. I invited him and his family over to my house for dinner, where our wives met for the first time.

The next day he stopped by the office for the customary "let's go meet the boss" introduction. He asked, "Joe, would you stay around the squadron and help me until you retire? All of this stuff is new to me." I immediately said yes, then I remembered the unique situation I was in.

I said, "You will have to get that approved by the chief of staff. If he says yes, of course I'll stay. I would love to work for you."

Because I was senior in rank to him, we both laughed at that statement. Traditionally, both the old and the new commanders would go see the supervisor. However, the tension between me and the chief of staff was so high that I did not want to see him and I knew he did not want to see me. So I called the captain into the office and asked him to escort the new squadron commander to meet the chief of staff, which he did.

When the commander returned from the meeting, he said, "Joe, I got some bad news. I asked the chief of staff if you could stay in the squadron during the transition period and he said no. He does not want you around the squadron at all anymore."

These comments really hurt me, even considering that they came from the warped mind of the chief of staff. I knew it wasn't anything I had done wrong; it was simply the color of my skin that generated his comments. The new commander felt very, very sorry but I told him not to. I had grown used to the new chief of staff's racist actions.

"It is not your fault," I explained. "After the change of command ceremony, I won't come to the squadron ever again."

Hearing that, the captain just hung his head in despair and walked out of my office.

The next day, I received a telephone call from the athletic director, who made me an interesting offer after he heard what the chief of staff was doing to me. "Joe, you have served the academy well and you deserve a better fate than that," he said. "Would you like to work for me until you retire?"

My spirits leapt. "That would be great, sir. I'll report to you the day after my change of command."

"No, go ahead and take a few days off. I'll see you here a few days afterwards."

"Thank you, sir," I replied with gratitude.

Thanks to him I was able to spend my final months in the Air Force working in the athletics department. He definitely prevented a major incident; I can't imagine what would have happened if I had had to spend those months as the chief of staff's trophy, like an animal he had captured and put on display for everyone to see. I was not going to be his "boy." I would have gone to jail first for insubordination.

A few days before the ceremony, I discussed it with Ruby. She was very upset at the whole situation, especially the bold racism that no one was willing to address. Ruby herself was no stranger to racism. She had been born and raised in Memphis, Tennessee, and she and her siblings spent their summers with their grandparents in Mississippi. Ruby's mother, Mrs. Sarah Kimbrough, was the strongest woman I have ever known. I admired her very much for surviving against all odds. Mrs. Sarah and her husband, Mr. Solomon Kimbrough, eloped to Memphis from Holly Springs, Mississippi, at the age of seventeen. They wanted a better life for their children. Ruby had one older brother, Solomon, Jr., and three sisters: Ernestine, Geraldine, and Bonnie.

Mr. Kimbrough worked in a factory for many years and Miss Sarah worked various jobs to help support their children. Ruby's brother, Solomon, Jr., served four years in the Air Force and when Memphis transit bus drivers were integrated, Junior was one of the first black drivers hired. Mrs. Kimbrough often told me about working three jobs at once because she had three children in college at the same time when Ernestine was studying at Tennessee State while Ruby and Geraldine were at Leyome-Owen College.

During Ruby's second year in college, her uncle, Joe, came to Memphis and took her back with him to attend college in San Francisco. All of the girls eventually graduated from college.

When I asked Ruby if she was going to the change of command ceremony, she gave me an emphatic, "No!" She reminded me that she had been with this Air Force for nineteen years and had been to probably hundreds of military and civilian functions, but she wasn't going to go to this one. "Joseph, I have supported your career and delayed my own, not for some racist commander like the chief of staff, and not for your career to end this way," she reminded me, pain etched onto her pretty face.

I knew she was right. Ruby had been the loyal Air Force officer's wife for many years. On various bases she had served in many positions in the Officer Wives Clubs, worked in Air Force Family Services, and on our previous assignment, she had served both as a volunteer counselor at the Social Actions office and president of the Air Force Family Services unit. While at the academy she hadn't worked in an official capacity, but still she had supported the Cadet Sponsorship program 100 percent. This would be the first time in nineteen years that she was refusing to attend a function with me.

"You have to be there; I don't. I am not going to watch you stand up tall for him," she argued.

I knew Ruby well enough to know not to force her to attend. Her mind was made up and, truthfully, if I did not have to attend, I would not have gone either. Our son, Brian, who was twelve years old at the time, overheard part of the conversation and asked if he could go to the ceremony. I looked at Ruby, asking for her permission.

"Yes," she said. "Take him along. Brian is too young to understand anyway. Also, you may take Patti and Teresa." Teresa is my twenty-two-year-old niece who was spending a few weeks with us after graduating from college.

On the afternoon of my last day as commander, as I cleaned out my desk and took my pictures and awards off the walls in my office, my secretary came into my office with tears in her eyes and asked if I needed any help. "Colonel, this isn't right," she pleaded.

"I know. But so far no one is willing to stop the chief of staff and the superintendent isn't willing to see me."

"Is Mrs. Hoffler coming to the change of command ceremony tomorrow?" Pat asked.

"No, she isn't coming," I replied.

"I didn't think so," she said. "Mrs. Hoffler is a strong black woman. She isn't going to put up with the new chief of staff's stuff. Colonel, as soon as you leave, the chief will get rid of me, too. But I am a Christian person and I know that the Lord will make this right one day. I pray that He will. You don't deserve this."

"Thank you," I replied, touched at the kindness of her words and hoping that she was right.

When the chief of staff arrived for the ceremony the following day, it was a very tense time in the building. Amazingly, this was the first time in five months, since he'd become chief of staff, that he visited the security police building. I did not want to speak to him, or even acknowledge his presence. I tried to avoid him as we both moved through the building, and I noticed that the black troops avoided him as well. They knew the score and did not want to be patronized by even speaking to him. Then again, he only seemed interested in talking to the white airmen, including the new commander and the chief.

When the first sergeant announced that it was time for the ceremony to begin, we all went outside and took our places. After I officially passed my command to the new commander, the chief of staff spoke to the squadron. I'll never forget his exact words, and neither would the members of my squadron.

"Lieutenant Colonel Hoffler has been here too long," he said. "He has been at the academy for five years and it's time that he move on. It's time for a change, and the new commander will bring that change." As my replacement was white, it became very obvious that he was implying a change in the color of the command element of the squadron.

It was an incredibly humiliating slap in the face to be spoken of in these terms in front of my airmen. After I gathered my thoughts, I thanked the squadron for their support. I said that I had enjoyed being their commander and hoped that they would support the new commander, just as they had supported me for the previous five years.

After the ceremony, we all went into the building for refreshments and while I was talking to the NCOIC security police operations, the chief of staff approached us. My son was standing beside me. The chief of staff put his hand on Brian's head and asked, "Joe, is this your son?"

I stared at him and replied, "Would you please remove your hand from my son's head?"

Then I took Brian by the hand and led him to another area of the building. That was July 17, 1984, and from that day on I never returned to the squadron. The captain and the first sergeant invited me back many times, but I could never face the troops again. On the way home, my niece Teresa said, "Uncle Joseph, I don't know much about the military, but wasn't that man supposed to say something good about you and your service to your country? Well, he did not. What was his problem?"

"Teresa, dear, one day you'll learn…hopefully from a distance…about people like him."

True to form, when the chief of staff was later questioned during my congressional inquiry, he claimed that he requested the change of command ceremony to highlight my accomplishments to the squadron. He also claimed that he never said anything embarrassing about me to my squadron. Both of those statements are lies. He wasn't even brave enough to tell the truth to the investigating officer.

After the change of command ceremony in July, I had another two months until September, before I would officially retire from the Air Force. It was a difficult period, working in the academy's athletics department and just waiting for my distinguished military career to end on such a sour note. In September I received a telephone call from the NCOIC of the Security Police Squadron orderly room. He sounded nervous and very upset.

"Sir, I just received a telephone call from the awards section in personnel and the sergeant told me that the chief of staff has declined your medal upon retirement," he said. It is standard procedure in the military to present awards to service members upon their retirement and he had assumed that the chief of staff would approve mine.

I was shocked.

"What do I do now, sir?" he asked.

My mind was racing. "Hold off on this for now and I will get back to you," I replied.

I called the captain and the first sergeant and told them what the NCOIC of the orderly room had said. They were both in disbelief. I said, "Enough of the chief of staff's b.s. This is blatant racism, and I'm going to file a discrimination complaint with the base Social Actions office."

So I called Headquarters Social Actions. (The Social Actions office was supposed to address reports of discrimination in the Air Force.) When I relayed my case to the officer in charge, he requested that I start with the base Social Actions office at the academy.

"The base social actions officer works for the chief of staff, who is the main culprit in this case," I explained. "There is no way he is going to fall on his sword for me."

"Sir, I cannot help you unless you go through your base Social Actions office first," the duty officer said.

So with much apprehension I dialed the base Social Actions office and asked to speak to the social actions officer whom I knew quite well. He and I had worked together on some projects in the past. Also I had worked previously with the NCOIC of social actions and the male civilian employee.

When I walked into the base Social Actions office, the civilian smiled and said that the major and the master sergeant were waiting for me in the conference room. To my surprise, when I entered the room the major said, "Colonel, I have been waiting for you. When I found out who was going to be the new chief of staff, I knew that eventually the two of you would bump heads."

"Actually, Major, we have bumped more than just heads. But more importantly, why were you expecting me?" I asked, confused.

"Well, I know the chief of staff," he replied.

"What does that mean?"

"I'd prefer just to leave it at that," he said uneasily.

"If you insist," I replied. "But if you are going to conduct an investigation that I'm requesting, it would help me to know everything that you know."

"Very well." He hesitated. "Colonel, at the last airmen's award banquet, my wife and I were seated at the table with the chief of staff and his wife. When the black sergeant in the academy band sang that love song to the white female airman, the chief of staff's spouse used a very unacceptable and demeaning term about him to her husband. As everyone at the table was white, she probably thought she was in 'safe' territory. The chief of staff tapped her arm as if to say, 'Not everyone at this table thinks that way. Leave that kind of talk at home.'"

The major looked embarrassed.

"So as the base social actions officer, what did you do when this happened?"

"Nothing," he admitted.

The major then informed me that any request for an investigation had to be in writing. The master sergeant attempted to get the major out of the hot seat and asked if he could do the investigation himself. The major said no, once he got my request in writing he would do the investigation.

The following day I gave the major my request in writing, in a document titled "Racial Discrimination by the Chief of Staff." My report contained references to instances of discrimination in several areas, including in the awarding of medals. Although the chief of staff had only been my supervisor for four months out of my five years at the academy, he denied me a medal upon retirement. However, he approved medals for two white lieutenant colonels who were retiring at the same time as me, even though both men had negative reports against them. One of the men had been AWOL for a week while the other had threatened an airman in his unit for making an inspector general report against him.

My report to the Social Actions office also detailed specifics of the chief of staff's witch hunt against me, including sending me a letter of reprimand via base distribution and allowing news of my "punishment" to leak out in an effort to further embarrass me. In addition, I mentioned that there had been a meeting of the top five black officers at the academy who were concerned about the racial climate there. I also mentioned that all of the three black officers who had worked for the chief of staff at the Air Force Academy had either curtailed their assignments or had them curtailed by him. Two black female officers who worked for him when he was the director of personnel curtailed their assignments because he treated them differently than their white counterparts. They had been assigned to work hidden away in the cadet area, rather than in the more visible personnel office where they would have been seen by base personnel. To my knowledge, no white officers who worked under him when he was the director of personnel curtailed their assignments during that time.

I also mentioned in my report that the chief of staff refused to allow me to extend my tour of duty for three months for the purpose of promotion potential, even though HQ Air Force had requested that extension.

A few days later the social actions officer called and informed me that a colonel who was now the director of personnel would be investigating my case. I immediately smelled a "rat." I asked the major, "Colonel who?"

After getting the answer, I replied, "No way. He is the chief of staff's close friend. How did he get chosen for this?"

The major had to tell the truth. "The chief of staff chose him."

"What?" I exploded.

It turned out that the social actions officer had unprofessionally briefed the chief of staff on my social action complaint. Now the chief of staff knew everything and could prepare for the questions. "Major, this is unacceptable," I said. The major admitted that because the chief of staff was his supervisor, he was afraid of him. I told the major that since he is white, he didn't have anything to worry about. I later discovered that the major and the chief of staff belonged to the same church. Nothing could further exhibit the double standard of black and white justice at the Air Force Academy. A white airman makes allegations against me and I cannot see them. I was never even advised that I was under investigation, nor could I see the investigation report to defend myself. A black lieutenant colonel makes an allegation against a white colonel and not only does the colonel get to see the allegations against him first, he even gets to choose his best friend as the investigating officer. So much for "color blind justice at the Air Force Academy."

During our phone conversation, the social actions officer explained that when he called for an appointment with the superintendent, the superintendent's secretary informed the chief of staff. So the chief of staff asked the social actions officer why he wanted to see the superintendent.

The major told him why and then showed him a copy of my complaint. The chief of staff then chose the director of personnel to be the investigating officer. At that point I demanded that the social actions officer properly do his job and brief the superintendent and have him appoint an investigating officer, rather than one appointed by the chief of staff, to investigate himself.

When I hung up the telephone, the captain entered my office. "Captain, the more I learn about the chief of staff, the more I realize that this person should not be in the U.S. Air Force and especially not at the academy, where the mission is to train the future leaders of the Air Force. He has no morals, no honesty, and no integrity and is a dyed-in-the-wool racist. He wanted to choose his own investigating officer."

"What is he afraid of?" the captain asked.

He shook his head, having never seen anything like this before. "Colonel H., somebody will stop this guy," he said softly. "Now that the superintendent is aware of what went on, I am sure he'll stop him and make everything all right."

"Captain, the chief of staff sits right outside the superintendent's office. Meanwhile I can't even get in to see him."

"Yeah, Colonel H., you are right there."

Following my request to take the director of personnel off as the investigator of my case, the superintendent appointed Colonel Philip Brothers to investigate my case. His investigation began September 1 and ended September 10. Col. Brothers was an interesting choice, being the first and only black permanent professor at the Air Force Academy. He had been named permanent professor during a different era. At that time the Air Force Academy had been concerned with diversity and the promotion of minority officers. As the senior black officer, he had unofficially served as a mentor to the other black officers at the Air Force Academy during my tenure there.

When Col. Brothers informed me that he would be investigating my complaint, I was relieved. To stay neutral, I connected the colonel with the first sergeant to help arrange interviews with the squadron personnel. Unlike the academy's investigating officer, who had interviewed only white security policemen in his zeal to build a case against me, Col. Brothers interviewed a variety of airmen of all races and all ranks within the squadron.

During the investigation, the first sergeant told the captain and me that his sources revealed that A1C Brett Stover's Airman Performance Report (APR) had been changed from a "seven" to a "nine" and had been signed by the chief of staff. To accomplish that feat, he had to have directed someone to enter the records section in the personnel branch and illegally remove A1C Stover's performance report from its folder then replace it with a new report with his signature. If a service member felt that his or her performance report was incorrect, the Air Force had a procedure whereby it could be challenged by that person. But an action such as the chief of staff's was illegal, very serious, and undermined the whole Air Force promotion/assignment system. His actions were further compounded by the fact that as the previous director of personnel, he knew better. He knew the proper procedure for correcting APRs. This was another example of how rules did not apply to the chief of staff and everyone in the academy was afraid to cross him. He was a very vindictive person and would use his position to get anyone who dared to go against him. The academy's inspector general was aware of this major infraction, but did nothing about it.

Armed with what I considered this "smoking gun," I gave the new information to Col. Brothers and asked that he investigate it. He agreed that it was very serious and was shocked that the chief of staff would go so far as to violate Air Force regulations concerning personnel records.

A few days later, Col. Brothers told me that he could not investigate the situation concerning the changing of A1C Stover's performance report after all. He said that the IG had told him that such an inquiry exceeded his authority. "What?" I asked in shock. "If not you, then who can investigate it?" Apparently no one investigated it. It was covered up by the "good ole boys." If someone had investigated it, the chief of staff, inspector general and director of personnel would have been fired from their positions.

"Apparently you need to contact the base inspector general," he answered.

"You've got to be kidding," I protested. "Right now the base inspector general is the previous investigating officer, the man who initiated this whole witch hunt against me! When he began investigating me, he threatened my airmen with disciplinary action if they did not give him the answers he wanted. He has blood on his hands. Now you want me to ask him to incriminate himself in the violation of official Air Force records?" I shook my head in disgust.

Col. Brothers conducted an inquiry into my social action complaint 1-10 in September 1984. A summary/excerpts of his inquiry are detailed below.

[Most individuals who were questioned by the inquiry officer, the USAF Academy's investigating officer] felt that he was only interested in testimony that would confirm a preconceived conclusion. In some instances, individuals returning from interviews were perplexed by the atmosphere or attitude with which they were questioned. In other cases, trying to become informed, they questioned other individuals about the nature of the inquiry. The whole situation affected morale in what the record shows is an outstanding unit.

Col. Brothers' conclusions were:

> a. *While the results of the actions taken against Lt. Col. Joseph W. Hoffler were unequal, I find no compelling evidence to conclude that decisions made were on the basis of his race.*
> b. *The IG investigation of fraud, waste and abuse was conducted in an unprofessional manner.*

c. Lt. Col. Hoffler is not completely blameless in these events. However, I conclude he was dealt with based on incomplete information.

The superintendent's inquiry officer concluded that the actions taken against me were unequal—that the investigation that ended my Air Force career was conducted in an unprofessional manner and based on incomplete information. What other proof did the Air Force need to invalidate that investigation? Yet the superintendent and the Air Force inspector general let the investigation stand.

No person can be blameless in events in which the preconceived conclusion is to find the person guilty of doing something over a five-year period. And the chief of staff did not have to justify his actions to anyone.

"Joe, there is nothing substantial in the USAF Academy's investigating officer's report," Col. Brothers acknowledged during that briefing. "It is obvious that they were just scaring you off to force you to retire without being promoted and to give the chief of staff justification to enter a negative item into your personnel file."

Additional details of the report revealed that the academy's investigating officer and the inspector general had intimidated witnesses into lying to support the chief of staff. For example:

a. A major from the legal office said he had never given permission to allow football pools when in fact he had.

b. The deputy IG denied coming down to my building to tell us that A1C Stover was weird and could not be trusted. When he came to the office to speak with my operations officer, he obviously did not know that the "fix" was on.

c. The base therapist accused the operations officer and first sergeant of forcing him to say that A1C Stover was unstable, which was not true. No one from the Security Police Squadron harassed the base therapist as claimed by the investigating officer. The base therapist initially performed his job according to Air Force regulations and evaluated A1C Stover's mental state as unstable.

However, under pressure from the USAF Academy's investigating officer and the USAF Academy inspector general, he changed his assessment of A1C Stover.

CHAPTER 14

MEETING WITH THE SUPERINTENDENT

A few days after the completion of Col. Brothers' report, I received a call from the superintendent's secretary saying that he wanted to see me in his office. *Great,* I thought. *At long last I will get a chance to voice my opinion to the superintendent.* However when I reported to the superintendent, he very sternly told me that he was approving me for a medal, not because I had earned one but because others who were not worthy had already been awarded them. I was shocked and requested permission to speak. He told me in no uncertain terms that he did not want to hear anything I had to say. He was furious at me for submitting a social action report about discrimination at the USAF Academy.

I also couldn't believe that after learning, through my social action complaint, that the top five black officers at the academy had earlier held a meeting about the academy's racial climate, he wasn't more concerned. After all, the credentials of the attendees at that meeting back in February 1984 could not have been more impeccable. Of the five black Air Force officers present, two were colonels and three were lieutenant colonels. Two held Ph.Ds and three had master's degrees. I would have expected the superintendent to reconvene the meeting in his office so that the concerns about the racial climate at the academy could be addressed directly to him. Instead he used his authority to sabotage that meeting by offering choice assignments and promotions to some of the attendees as a form of appeasement. Not only that, here he was summoning me to his office, doing all the talking and then telling me directly, "I don't want to hear anything you have to say. You are dismissed." It was clear that my filing a social action complaint hit a nerve with him.

After my meeting with the superintendent, I rushed home to tell Ruby about the new developments. She was happy that there was going to be a retirement ceremony, but clearly upset about the medal. "Will you attend my retirement?" I asked.

"Will the chief of staff be there?" she asked warily.

"No."

"Okay. Then I will go," Ruby said. "What else happened in the meeting? Did you get the chance to tell him your side of the story?"

"No," I explained. "He told me he didn't want to hear anything from me and that he had heard enough about this. I couldn't believe it. He wouldn't let me say a word."

Ruby was dismayed. "You mean to tell me that a black lieutenant colonel with twenty-two years of commendable service cannot speak to his commander to clear himself of trumped-up charges? But a white airman with all kinds of negative items in his file can do whatever he wants? The top officers at the academy believe him over you; he had access to the chief of staff and the inspector general but no one talks to you."

"Yes, that is correct," I said.

Ruby became very emotional. "Joseph, this is what it has come down to—a matter of black and white."

The following day I told the captain, the first sergeant and the two master sergeants about my conversation with the superintendent.

"Did you get a chance to mention that the chief of staff changed A1C Stover's performance report?" the captain asked eagerly.

"No," I replied, shaking my head. "He did not want to hear a word from me. He made that perfectly clear. When a three-star general tells you to leave his office, you leave."

"This is a sad Air Force," the NCOIC security police operations said, "when an airman who has been on base less than one year, who cannot perform the duty he is assigned, and who has a seven APR, receives more credibility than a lieutenant colonel with twenty-two years of service and all top-rated performance reports. Now, someone tell me that race is not a factor in this situation."

"Race is a factor," I acknowledged. "And it looks as if it is the only factor. It's like Ruby said to me this morning, 'It's all come down to a matter of black and white.'"

After discussing with the captain my frustrating lack of progress in getting my case heard, he suggested that I contact my senator. I said, "I am from North Carolina. Do you really think my senator is going to fight for me in a case involving incidents of racial discrimination?"

The captain then suggested that I contact the senator from Colorado, Senator Armstrong, which I did in October 1984. Senator Armstrong's office was in Denver and the captain insisted on accompanying me to the meeting, even though I advised him not to. I reminded him that he was still on active duty at the academy and based on current trends, if someone at the academy discovered that he had accompanied me to request a congressional inquiry against the academy, he might face serious career repercussions. He smiled widely. "Colonel H., I have been with you this far, I need to go. I'm supporting you all the way."

It wasn't easy for me to request a congressional inquiry against the Air Force; however, I felt that something had to be done. The chief of staff had corrupted the Air Force's own system and for justice, I had to go outside that system.

While all this was going on I never discussed the details of the investigation with the NCOIC security police operations and the NCOIC of security investigation. The main reason I didn't was pride. As a proud black Air Force officer and commander, it was hard for me to admit that the institution that I loved and had served for twenty-two years had wronged me. A policy that I had long advocated to others in the Air Force was, "Work hard and the Air Force will do its part to protect you from discrimination." After I was relieved of my duties as commander and my public "lynching" could no longer be hidden, the NCOIC security police operations and I had a serious and important discussion. We concluded that for both of us, our only crime was being black. The chief of staff apparently wanted to "get" us both. Having gotten me, he turned his attention to destroying the Air Force career of the NCOIC security police operations also.

I received a phone call from the NCOIC security police operations in September. After me, he was the highest-ranking black in the Security Police Squadron. He sounded very upset as he asked if we could meet somewhere private to talk. I was no longer his commander and was working for the athletics department at that point, so I did not have access to a private office. Instead I suggested that we meet someplace in the athletics area, like the basketball arena. When he and I got to the arena we took our seats in the empty stands, sitting up high where no one could overhear us. A few cadets were shooting baskets on the floor but the stands were empty so we could talk in private.

He was very upset and emotional, which was unusual for him. He told me that his new commander had stripped him of his position as NCOIC of operations and gave him a letter of reprimand.

I was shocked. "What did you do in such a short period of time to deserve a LOR?"

He took a deep breath as he relayed the story. "Colonel, do you remember the incident that happened that night at the NCO Club in June? When I was accused of throwing a beer bottle at a passing car?"

"Of course. But the ops officer investigated that report and found it without credibility."

The NCOIC security police operations and the security police investigator had been there on a stakeout on a case and a civilian had accused him of throwing a beer bottle at her passing car. His investigation showed that the female civilian made the accusation in order to cover up the fact that she was in a car with a sergeant who was not her husband. The woman realized that the NCOIC security police operations recognized her because her husband was in the security police Squadron. "You and I have spoken about that incident. I advised you to be more careful when you are at the NCO Club on a case."

He nodded. "And Colonel, do you remember that the chief wanted you to give me a letter of reprimand because of that incident?"

"Yes," I replied, "but the captain and I told him how ridiculous that request was."

"Well, my commander told me that the chief of staff 'reopened' the case, determined that I was guilty, and directed that I receive a LOR."

"What do you mean 'reopened' the case? Did he interview you or any other witnesses?"

"Of course not, sir. He just demanded that I get a LOR."

"Wait a minute. How did he find out about that case, which happened over four months ago?"

"I guess the chief told him about it. That is the only way the chief of staff could have found out. Colonel, for African-Americans, this place, this so-called 'academy' is nothing more than an old-fashioned plantation." He shook his head in disgust.

I was taken aback by that shocking analogy. "Wait a minute. The day shift flight chief recently used that same term to describe the Air Force Academy."

"We call it a plantation because it is," he explained. "You see that here, we serve at the mercy of the white man. We have no rights. Look at you, a squadron commander, a lieutenant colonel, you contacted the HQ Social Actions, base Social Actions and HQ IG and you can't even get in to talk to your commander? What am I, just a master sergeant, going to do? So tell me, sir, isn't this just like a plantation? We African-Americans have no rights here and we're treated like nothing more than slaves." He looked up at me sadly. "I did not accept the LOR, but it doesn't matter, because Chief of Staff Smith reopened the case even though it was investigated and closed before he became chief of staff, and directed discipline toward me."

"I'm so sorry. I don't know what to say."

He took a deep breath. "At first, Colonel, I blamed you for this happening."

"Why is that?" I asked, taken aback.

"Because you asked me to come to the academy to assist you," he explained. "But then I realized that this wasn't your fault. They got you, too. The chief of staff and the chief are working together. Both are racists and no one will stop them."

I shook my head in disgust. "Now that they have disciplined and removed from positions of authority the two senior African-Americans in the squadron, they are probably having a celebration party."

"Colonel, do you think Jimmy is safe?" he asked with concern. Jimmy is a junior master sergeant who is black.

"Oh, yeah, Jimmy is safe," I said. "They just wanted you and me out of the way. He isn't seen as a threat to their white supremacy theory. I was the commander and you were the NCOIC of operations, so there was a lot of power centered in those positions."

"Colonel, did you know that during that investigation, Jimmy went to see the chief of staff to defend you and he told him to leave his office?"

"Yeah, the captain told me about it."

"The chief of staff agreed to see Jimmy, but when he began saying positive things about you and the squadron, the chief of staff told him that was enough. Jimmy told me that the chief of staff obviously only wanted to hear negative things about you and not anything positive." We paused to watch the cadets playing basketball on the floor beneath us.

"Colonel, I have known you since 1976 when you first arrived at RAF Mildenhall," he said wistfully. "I remember the first day seeing my first black Security Police Squadron commander and the talk that was going on around the squadron, that we have a black commander. And how proud we were of you. That name, Hoffler, really threw everyone for a curve!" He smiled at that recollection. "But you showed them, sir," he continued. "The squadron went from a 'marginal' to an 'excellent' rating in three years. I'm sure that just like here at the academy, some of the white members at RAF Mildenhall did not like working for a black commander, but unlike here, the people at Mildenhall put their jobs first and their racial prejudices second."

"At RAF Mildenhall, I had a great staff working for me and we all worked together. Plus I had outstanding support at the base and wing commanders levels. However, here at the academy, there was always something about that squadron that made me uncomfortable. I always felt like I was peddling upstream."

"I know the reason, sir. It's Chief Michaels; he was stabbing you in the back every chance he got. When Director of Personnel Smith became the chief of staff, it seems like the two of them, especially the chief, brought their white sheets and hoods out of the closet." We both laughed a little at that comment. "Colonel, I had a friend stationed with the chief at his last base. He called me one day and said that we, meaning the black airmen, would be sorry that the chief was in our squadron. My friend called him the biggest racist he had ever met in the Air Force and also said that to get rid of him, the commander at his last assignment eliminated his slot. Then he ended up assigned here at the academy."

"I guess this is partly my fault," I admitted. "I wanted a chief for the squadron and he was the only one available."

"It doesn't look like it's over for either of us," he said. "What's next?"

"Well, the captain has suggested a congressional meeting with Senator Armstrong's staff in Denver."

"The captain arranged it?" He sounded surprised.

"That's right. Meeting with a member of a senator's staff never occurred to me before. I never expected that I would have to request a congressional inquiry on my supervisor. I always thought that the Air

Force would take care of business. But now it seems that where the Air Force Academy is concerned, image comes first. We tried everything within the Air Force itself and now it is time to go outside of it."

"At least you've got the captain watching your back," he said. "Colonel, I have never met a white person like him before."

"Neither have I," I admitted. "He could have just sat back, let the higher-ups hang me out to dry and then take my job, but he didn't. He keeps fighting and fighting for justice."

"Sir, at this point I don't have any faith in the Air Force anymore."

"I don't either. But I do have faith in the United States government to hold the Air Force accountable for their actions. For now, all we can do is wait and see."

Then, for the first time, I told the NCOIC security police operations all the details of my case. I had told the captain and first sergeant but not the black NCOs in the squadron. "Let me explain what happened to me. For more than twenty years I told minority service members that if they worked hard, they would make it in the Air Force. I told them that the Air Force, like every other military branch, had its share of racists, but the establishment itself would not tolerate racism. What I meant was that a person might not like African-Americans, but he would be afraid to discriminate against a black person for fear of the consequences.

"But now I realize that I was wrong. It's hard for me to look you guys in the face and admit that I have been wrong for more than twenty years."

Then I told him the whole story about how I had been set up, first by the academy's investigating officer, who called me in to speak to me without ever revealing that I was under investigation, no Article 31 rights advisement. He found me guilty of gambling with enlisted troops, which I never did, and stealing a small piece of Plexiglas, which was given to me as scrap.

"Gambling with troops?" The NCOIC security police operations sounded amazed. "Colonel, remember those times when we were visiting the pass and ID room and we had to pass by the personnel conference room? They had baby shower raffles, baby shower drawings, World Series pools, Super Bowl pools, etc. Things like that are all over the academy. So why are you the only commander being disciplined for allowing football pools?"

"Because I'm black and the chief of staff wants to get rid of me," I replied.

I went on to explain how the chief of staff waited until I was visiting my sick brother to have the investigating officer start questioning my troops. Then he suggested that I retire, followed by the letter of reprimand that arrived via base distribution.

"I guess that the chief of staff was sending the squadron a message," he surmised.

"No, two messages. The first message was to the blacks in the squadron, letting them know that no matter how high your rank, a white man can take you down. You best just stay in your place. The second message was to the white airmen, saying, 'Hey, if you don't want to work for a black commander or NCO, give me some dirt on him, I'll find him guilty and publicly discipline him.'"

He nodded and looked down at the basketball court. "Well, Colonel, I feel better now having had this conversation. At first I blamed you for what's happening to me, and then I blamed myself. Now I realize that it is neither one of us. We're only guilty of being black."

"It is all the Air Force's fault for letting the chief of staff use his racism to destroy two careers."

"I hope that you and the captain have success in your meeting with Senator Armstrong," he offered.

I nodded. "Well, it can't get any worse than it is now. Ron, as we are talking about racial discrimination in the military, let me paraphrase a statement from Eleanor Roosevelt, who led the fight for racial equality for blacks during World War II. In fact, the Tuskegee Airmen probably would not have been given a chance if it had not been for her support. She said, 'You cannot embarrass me without my consent.' Well, the chief of staff has done everything in his power to embarrass me. At the change of command ceremony, he even made harmful remarks about me in front of my family, friends and squadron."

Ron said, "Sir, you are so right. I remember the comments. I could not believe my ears. I asked myself why he would say those negative things about you. Colonel, that had to be hard for you to take."

"Ron, this whole situation never was about disciplining. It was no coincidence that the two senior blacks in the squadron received letters of reprimand. It was about some whites in the squadron complaining to the chief of staff and inspector general about too many blacks in senior positions. It was about the chief of staff denying me promotion to colonel because he knew I had the records and about him attempting to publicly embarrass the only black officer in his agency. But Ron, he cannot embarrass me, because I am not giving him my consent. I will fight him all the way."

"Colonel, that sounds like something I would expect you to say." He paused then added, "I am going to retire. I put my papers in earlier when I saw what was happening to you. My wife is home, buying the land and making plans for a house."

"When you talk to her, give her my regards," I said.

"Thank you, Colonel, for teaching me and Jimmy how to play golf. Now I have something to do in my retirement." We both laughed.

"Colonel, for many years I watched the white commanders and airmen play golf together while I was working. I often wondered if that would ever happen to me. Jimmy said the same thing. We never thought we would have a commander who would care enough to teach us how to golf. Some troops told me that seeing the three of us playing golf together used to really burn up the chief." I smiled at his recollection. He continued, "I guess you'll have to find another foursome for bid whist, now that they have broken that also."

"Yes, I guess I will." 'Bid whist' is a card game, similar to bridge, that is played mostly by African-Americans. "You should have let me teach you and Jimmy how to play bridge."

"That's okay, sir," he responded. "Where I am going in Tennessee, there won't be any need for bridge. They only play bid whist there." We laughed again, then stood up, hugged, and shook hands for a very emotional goodbye.

Although he said he had forgiven me for asking him to come to the academy, I still felt sad and responsible, as if I had unwittingly destroyed an outstanding Air Force career.

I only saw him one more time and that was at my retirement ceremony. He left the academy a few weeks after I did. Six years later, I received a phone call from his wife, sharing the sad news that he had passed away from cancer. She believed he had been exposed to Agent Orange while stationed in Vietnam. It was a sad end to a fine life, and a sad memory of what was an outstanding career cut short by racism.

CHAPTER 15

FACING EARLY RETIREMENT

When talk in the squadron turned to my upcoming retirement ceremony, I felt torn between having a full retirement ceremony or forgoing the whole event entirely. I told my staff that I did not want to retire without the proper ceremony befitting my twenty-two years of outstanding service. But the captain and first sergeant would not take "no" for an answer.

"Sir," they said, "you are going to retire properly. We know that the chief of staff's actions against you have nothing to do with your job performance and everything to do with your race. Plus, sir, the troops have presentations for you, so please don't disappoint them."

"Very well then," I said. "I don't want to let my troops down."

So the first sergeant reserved the NCO Club for September 30 for my retirement ceremony. I wanted the ceremony there rather than at the Officers' Club for many reasons but primarily because I had started my Air Force career as an airman and I always felt a special connection to the enlisted personnel.

Following Col. Brothers' investigation that proved that the chief of

149

staff's actions against me were discriminatory, the superintendent approved my recommendation for the Air Force Meritorious Service Medal. Now, I had to find someone to award the medal to me. I obviously did not want my supervisor, the chief of staff, to present it, and the superintendent, my commander, had denied my request to retire me.

Unbelievably, the chief of staff actually asked that he be allowed to present me with my medal at my retirement ceremony. I couldn't believe that he had that kind of nerve. After the comments he had made at my change of command ceremony and after giving me that undeserved letter of reprimand and initially trying to deny me the medal, he said he wanted to present that same medal to me. What unbelievable gall. Clearly, this was a man with no sense of shame.

I said, "Absolutely no" to his request. I told the personnel sergeant, "Not only do I not want to be in the same room as the chief of staff, I don't want to be on the same planet with him."

My commander, the superintendent, was invited to attend the ceremony but declined. Interestingly enough, both he and the chief of staff attended the chief's retirement when the time came, less than a year later.

I asked Col. Brothers to retire me and present my medal at the ceremony. He and his spouse were my longtime friends since I first arrived at the academy and were mentors to the black officers there. He graciously agreed but expressed sadness that I was leaving the Air Force under such circumstances.

He said, "Joe, you know you had the records to get promoted."

"Yes, I know I did," I replied. "Prior to the chief of staff's and the inspector general's actions, I did."

On the morning of September 30, 1984, my last day on active duty, I put on my uniform for the very last time and stood looking at my proud reflection in the full-length mirror.

"Ruby, how do I look?" I asked.

Ruby let out a little laugh. "Your tie needs to be straightened." She walked over, straightened it, checked out my ribbons and ensured that my rank was straight on my uniform. "Colonel," she had never called me 'Colonel' before, "you really look sharp this morning. It is a shame that the Air Force is losing such an outstanding officer."

She had tears in her eyes as I reached down and stroked her cheek. I wrapped my arms around her and held her close.

"I know, but I cannot fight the racism at the academy anymore." I sighed. "My time has run out. I've got to move on and find new venues for fighting my case." With heavy hearts we put the kids in the car and drove to the NCO Club for the retirement ceremony.

The ceremony was well attended by members of the squadron, other units on the base, and civilian police forces that I had worked with over the years. My counterparts from Fort Carson, Peterson Air Force Base and HQ SPACECOM also attended. The many sections of the squadron presented me with many items of remembrance and memorabilia. The Base Logistic Squadron presented me with the valued "Greyhound Bus" trophy; the Cadet Wing presented me with their "Sword of Honor" for supporting the cadets; and the athletics department presented me with a plaque from the Air Force Academy football team.

As we drove out of the academy grounds after the ceremony, my heart sank as I realized that a huge part of my life was over. I was still a relatively young man at the age of forty-four but I had dedicated half of those forty-four years to serving my country in a military that now found me expendable, and all because I am black.

Even after my official retirement from the Air Force, I continued my quest for justice. Even if it was too late to salvage my own career, I felt I had a solemn duty to make sure that no other black Air Force officer had to suffer the way that I had.

When the captain and I arrived at Senator Armstrong's office in Denver, we made it very clear that due to possible repercussions against the captain, he was not officially there with me. He was only there for moral support and to confirm my information. I detailed to Jo Ann, the senator's staff member, my complaint of racial discrimination and tampering with Air Force records by the chief of staff. I also explained the harassment

The symbolic last salute from my first sergeant (right foreground), as TSgt. Johnnie Ravenell (center) looks on along with Ruby and Brian behind the first sergeant.

Members of the squadron who wanted a last picture with their commander—for all, the first black Air Force commander they served under. Left to right: SSgt. Leon Mallory, SSgt. Willie Mayes, Sgt. Patricia Mallory, Lt. Col. Joseph Hoffler, MSgt. Bobbie Hayes and MSgt. Rondell Jennings.

of my airmen by the investigating officer and the failure to perform the duties of inspector general of the academy by the USAF Academy inspector general. As the captain and I shared the details, Jo Ann could not believe that such actions were going on not only in today's military, but at the Air Force Academy, the very institution tasked with the duty to train the Air Force's future officers. She seemed very upset that a black serviceman who had served his country honorably for twenty-two years would have to endure such racism and prejudice. She even apologized for the Air Force and promised to look into the situation.

On our drive back to Colorado Springs, the captain and I were cautiously optimistic that based on our face-to-face meeting with Senator Armstrong's staff member, we had achieved justice at last. We "high-fived" each other and celebrated by stopping at an upscale restaurant on the way home. While waiting for our meals I phoned Ruby, who had been waiting anxiously at home for the news.

"Ruby," I said. "It went very well. It looks like I will finally have justice. Senator Armstrong is going to open a congressional inquiry into my allegations. The truth will come out at last. Surely the Air Force Academy can't influence a congressional inquiry."

"Joseph, that's wonderful. You have suffered enough. Now hurry home, dear. I'm preparing your favorite meal, great northern beans."

I looked sheepishly away from the phone. "That's okay, dear don't bother, I told her that the captain and I are celebrating at a nice restaurant. I really believe that things are starting to go my way."

In December, I received a telephone call from the HQ USAF investigating officer, informing me that he had been appointed to conduct the congressional inquiry that I had requested. He and I arranged to meet at the academy in a set of offices across from the inspector general's office. The HQ USAF investigating officer was stationed at Peterson AFB, which was located in the southeast section of Colorado Springs, approximately twelve miles away from the academy. At first he was very professional and proclaimed that he was going to conduct an impartial investigation. Unlike my initial meeting with the USAF Academy's investigating officer, the HQ USAF investigating officer had an assistant present who recorded all our comments.

Meanwhile, the first sergeant told me that his contacts at A1C Stover's new base in Texas told him that Stover was bragging about getting his old commander fired and was trying to pull some of the same things at his new base, where his new commander promptly discharged him.

"Unbelievable," I initially said. Then I thought to myself, *Why not? He pulled it off once, so why not again?* He was able to get one commander fired by lying and submitting false allegations, so he had nothing to lose. However, what A1C Stover failed to realize is that he was being used by the chief of staff and inspector general at the academy to "whiten" the command element of the Security Police Squadron by firing the black commander. They did not really believe his allegations. He served a purpose. He will never again get that high-level support.

Shortly afterwards, I received a telephone call from a police recruiter from a city in Texas. He was visiting the academy following up on A1C Stover's job application. It turned out that following his early discharge from the Air Force, Stover had applied for a position with the city's police department. The recruiter, who was an ex-security policeman himself, told me that he was suspicious of any applications from prior service applicants when he or she does not list their first sergeant and their commander as references. The squadron's first sergeant and commander are the persons who know more about their personnel than anyone else.

"So what is it with this Brett Stover?" the recruiter asked. "He was bragging to me about getting his commander fired while working undercover for the academy's inspector general. He was really proud of what he did. Stover was weird. Never saw anyone like him before."

The first sergeant and I were honest with the recruiter and told him the whole truth about Stover. The recruiter seemed shocked.

"Couldn't the brass see that something was seriously emotionally wrong with Stover?" the recruiter asked. "I noticed that he was strange during the first five minutes of our interview. No way I would issue this guy a weapon."

"Well, A1C Stover served a purpose," I explained. "The higher-ups used him to help them get rid of a black commander and replace him with one who was white."

The recruiter was even more shocked than before. "Colonel Hoffler, I just met you over the telephone. You seem like a great commander to me. All of your troops that I spoke to had high regard for you. It's really a shame that something like this could happen in today's military. I hope that the congressional inquiry corrects a serious wrong. I wish I could have worked for you when I was in the Air Force."

"Thank you. Those words mean a lot to me now."

In those early days just after my retirement, I often asked myself if there was anything I could have done differently or better that might have given me a more positive outcome. Perhaps I should have been more verbal when the racism first reared its ugly head.

But when the investigation first began I thought it would disappear as soon as the chief of staff learned the true reason for Stover's IG complaint and the methods used by the investigating officer. I limited the dissemination of information to the captain and the first sergeant because we thought we could end things right there. We saw no reason to spread dirt on something that we assumed would be over quickly.

Initially, I had no idea that the "fix" was on and that no matter what happened, I was going to be found guilty. Even while I was trying to keep the information about the investigation under control, the chief of staff was busy spreading it around the base, trying to embarrass me.

On May 23, 1984, I received a letter from the HQ USAF Academy. I was thrilled to receive it because I knew that it signaled the end of the congressional investigation. But when I opened the letter, I was shocked to see that it was from the superintendent at the USAF Academy.

My shock only increased when I read the letter and it stated that, due to the results of the Headquarters IG congressional investigation, which found that I had acted unprofessionally, the Meritorious Service medal that I had received at my retirement was being rescinded. Of course there were no details. What was I accused of? What was the evidence against me? There was no chance for me to explain my side of the story. Again, as with the chief of staff's letter of reprimand, as a black officer, I was not worthy of being talked to as a person.

A white airman, A1C Stover, had access to the command section, but I did not. I was so shocked that I literally could not speak for several moments.

"Joseph! Joseph, what's wrong?" Ruby asked, seeing my glazed expression.

It took a while for me to choke out an explanation. I realized that I had been naïve to think that the Air Force inspector general would conduct a full and fair inspection of the USAF Academy and, specifically, address the actions of the chief of staff. When at last I regained my voice I phoned the captain, who shared my shock and dismay.

"But Colonel H., when I spoke with the USAF investigating officer he seemed concerned about the alteration to Stover's APR, and the academy inspector general's investigating officer badgering witnesses and the inspector general telling me to stay out of it because they only wanted Joe."

"All I can think is that someone pressured the HQ USAF investigating officer, to protect the Air Force Academy. Captain, my only recourse at this point is to get a copy of that report."

"How are you going to do that?" he asked.

"I don't know but I will find out."

I wrote to the inspector general office in Washington, D.C., and under the Freedom of Information Act, I requested a copy of the investigation. They asked for a charge of $250.00 for reproduction costs, which I immediately mailed to them.

A few months later I received my Xerox box of documents and called the captain over to my house to review them. As we pored over the information, we were shocked. It was obvious that the USAF investigating officer had changed directions during his investigation and begun to investigate me as a reprisal for filing the IG complaint. Then the captain and I contacted Jo Ann in Senator Armstrong's office and told her about the outcome of the investigation. She also seemed very upset and said that she would check on something and get back to me. A week or so later she called back and said that the USAF had made their final determination in the case and there wasn't much more she could do about it.

"Apparently, the United States Air Force Academy doesn't have to answer to anyone: senator, congressman, or anyone else," I told the captain. "As a minority and a member of the Armed Forces you serve at your own risk. If you should happen to have a bigoted supervisor like the chief of staff, no one and no agency will defend you. The reputation of the Air Force Academy comes first, and enforcement of federal laws against racial discrimination and violation of one's constitutional rights to be advised that he or she is the subject of an investigation comes second."

Later in 1985, I noticed that blacks at the Air Force Academy were being promoted to positions and in rank that would have been unlikely a year earlier. While my investigation was going on, Lt. Col. Slade, a black professor, accepted a year's assignment to the Washington, D.C., area. During the promotion cycle in which the chief of staff robbed me of my promotion, both Lt. Col. Slade and the academy's investigating officer were promoted to colonel.

This ensured that the professor would not be around to assist me in my quest to fight discrimination at the academy in Colorado Springs. Following his year in D.C., he was promoted and returned to the academy as commandant of the preparatory school, a position he would never have been considered for if he had supported my charge of discrimination at the academy.

In March 1985, the captain informed me that another professor, Lt. Col. Louis, who had also been at that meeting of black officers in February 1984, had just been named the new academy inspector general.

He had been very militant about the treatment of black officers at the academy and his appointment surprised me because I knew that his appointment hadn't been in the works before my social actions complaint. I assumed that either he was also being "paid off" for not supporting me, just as the other professor had been, or else this represented a genuine effort on the part of the superintendent to transfer black officers to visible positions.

In my own personal view these Lt. Cols. Slade and Louis "sold out" to advance their own careers. The more I thought about these events the more I came to feel that I had been betrayed by my fellow black officers, who I thought were my friends at the academy. When I wrote my racial discrimination complaint to the Social Actions office, I mentioned the meeting held in February by the senior black officers at the academy, a meeting that was requested by the first black professor. His concern was that he was being "passed over" for a permanent professor's position. I had of course supported him during that meeting in February 1984 so I naturally looked for support from him during my investigation. However, when I learned that Lt. Col. Slade had been transferred to the Pentagon in Washington, D.C., I became suspicious.

Further research into his quick departure from the academy revealed that the superintendent, when briefed on the situation, had contacted the professor's supervisor, the dean of faculty, and arranged for him to transfer to Washington with the promise that if he kept quiet, he would be promoted and returned to the academy in one year.

When I discovered that he had transferred to the Pentagon, I phoned and told him what was happening to me and that things had not changed at the academy for the black officers for whom we had been fighting. I also asked why he left without saying goodbye. He replied that he did not have time because his stint at the Pentagon was a "short-notice" assignment. But his family had stayed behind in Colorado Springs, which was to me a sure sign that he planned to return. I asked him to provide me with a statement confirming that the meeting had been held in February discussing the feelings of black officers at the academy about the unfair treatment they were receiving. He tried to wiggle out of the conversation and it seemed that he wasn't as supportive as he had previously been.

As the academy's inspector general, Lt. Col. Louis would be the contact person for my congressional report. On several occasions, I called him for an appointment to discuss the findings of the report and the decision of the HQ USAF investigating officer.

The academy inspector general, Lt. Col. Louis, never returned my telephone calls and he gave the impression that he wanted nothing to do with me. And when Lt. Col. Slade returned to the academy, it was noticeable that I was like the "black plague," to be avoided at all cost. How painful when I considered that if I had not made my complaint about racial discrimination at the academy to Social Actions and to my senator from Colorado, Lt. Col. Slade would not have been promoted to colonel and Lt. Col. Louis would not have been named the academy inspector general. Those were both appeasement assignments and they worked. Once Lt, Cols. Slade and Louis received their rewards, they stopped expressing concerns about the situation of blacks at the academy.

The whole problem with racial discrimination at the academy can be traced to the lack of sensitivity of the superintendent to the plight of black service personnel. Also he was obviously perceived as weak by his subordinates, the chief of staff and the inspector general. Otherwise they would not have run amok violating people's rights, lying, illegally changing official records, and transferring personnel to other bases to cover their actions. When he was first informed that black officers were concerned about their lack of numbers and influence at the academy, the superintendent did nothing to address the situation beyond rewarding these two senior black officers for keeping quiet in my case. When the superintendent was informed by his investigating officer that every black officer who worked for the chief of staff in both of his assignments at the academy had problems with him, he did nothing to address it.

Among the black officers who had problems with the chief of staff were the two black female captains who decided to curtail their assignments. That alone should have caused concern for the superintendent.

Having the USAF Academy on one's record was considered a bonus when it came to promotions, so one wouldn't curtail an assignment there unless it was for very serious reasons.

And then, of course, my complaint against the chief of staff should have created some concern on the superintendent's part, particularly since I was the only black squadron commander at the academy. This meant also that I was the only black officer at his staff meetings. Approximately thirty-five officers attended those meetings and I was one of only three officers who regularly briefed the staff on disciplinary incidents, traffic accidents and other violations. The superintendent had endorsed an "outstanding" performance report for me just nine days before the chief of staff and the inspector general began their witch hunt against me. I know that he could have stopped the whole process and investigated what was really going on if he had chosen to do so. Obviously, the chief of staff and the inspector general thought that the superintendent was weak and that they could get away with it, and they were right. They would never have tried such actions under the previous superintendent.

CHAPTER 16

MY LIFE AFTER
THE AIR FORCE

As I moved deeper and deeper into my task of finding justice, I tried to pursue new and different avenues of possibility. When I first contacted Senator Armstrong, his office staff had been really great. They felt that what had happened to me was wrong and they wanted to change it. However, they ran up against the traditional roadblock that shoots up when someone makes a congressional complaint against the USAF Academy.

In hopes of getting around this catch-22, and since Ruby was from Memphis, Tennessee, we contacted her representative in Congress, Rep. Harold Sr. We hoped that as an African-American member of Congress he would be more sensitive to racial discrimination in the armed forces. Unfortunately, his office did absolutely nothing for my case. They readily accepted the Air Force's spin on the situation that I was a bad officer who deserved the treatment I had received.

Also in 1985, increasingly frustrated as more doors closed in my face and I began to lose hope, I sent packages to the NAACP Joint Center for Political Studies and the Rainbow Coalition; I never received a response

161

from either group. Apparently racial discrimination in the military wasn't high on their lists of priorities.

After I retired from the Air Force I found myself out of a job at the relatively young age of forty-four. I was a regular officer and had planned on being a thirty-year man. I was determined to continue my fight for justice, but I knew I needed to develop new skills and abilities if I planned to stay competitive in the working world.

Deciding that I needed some training in the emerging field of computers, on October 1, 1984, I enrolled at Colorado Technical College (CTC), studying computer science. Ruby and our children were very supportive of me developing new skills and experiences, hoping that would ease my transition into civilian life.

During my first semester at CTC I took a course in technical writing and really enjoyed it. That led me to obtain a job as a technical writer with a defense contractor, National System and Research (NS&R). During my two years at NS&R, I also worked as the alternate security officer, because my first love remained the field of security. After normal business hours and on weekends, I spent time at the office studying industrial security manuals and procedures.

Industrial security for a defense contractor was a far cry from the way the military protected and controlled classified information. The civilian contractor world had new regulations and was much more stringent on controls of classified material than the military had been, a very sobering realization for me after so many years in the armed forces. As much as I enjoyed my new job as a technical writer, as with most retired military people, I missed the camaraderie of being in a military unit. Fortunately, my co-workers helped to fill that void.

My supervisor at NS&R was Bob McGee, a retired Air Force major from Mississippi. I could not have asked for a better or fairer supervisor. One of the secretaries who worked at NS&R, Faye Gregory, who is white, had a very Southern accent.

"Faye, where are you from?"

"North Carolina," she replied.

"Really? Where in North Carolina?"

"Elizabeth City."

"Well, I'm from Hertford."

"I'm really from Hertford, too," she chuckled. "But since Hertford is so small, I usually just tell people that I'm from Elizabeth City."

So here we were, a black man and a white woman, from the same small town in North Carolina, working for the same small company way out in Colorado.

Unbelievable!

After that, Faye and I became fast friends. We were "homeboy and homegirl." She had even graduated from Perquimans High School. But since there were many years difference in our ages, all we had in common was a deep love for Hertford, its special pit barbecue and the surrounding area. Whenever one of us would go home for a visit, we would always bring back some Hertford barbecue and invite the other one over for a meal.

Even after I left NS&R I maintained my friendship with Faye and it continues to this day. It's always amazing for me to think that while growing up in the segregated South of the 1940s and 1950s, a friendship like the one that Faye and I had developed never could have happened.

When my contract with NS&R ended after just two years, I applied for a job as the facility security officer at another defense contractor, ARINC. In the interview room there were five people applying for the coveted position—four white applicants and me. The manager and the person making the selection was Harold "Hal" Townend. A few days after my interview, I received a call from Townend letting me know that I'd gotten the job. With my experiences at the Air Force Academy still so fresh in my mind, I was admittedly somewhat surprised that I received the job over four white applicants.

One day in August 1987, Spike, a retired Air Force major who worked at ARINC, approached me in the hallway and said, "Joe, you seem very knowledgeable about sports and you're fun to be around. A group of ARINC employees are planning to purchase season tickets for the Air Force Academy football games and we would like to know if you and Ruby want to join us." He paused. "If we bought them now, we could get seats together."

"Thanks, Spike, but no, I really don't want to attend football games at the academy this year," I replied.

Spike said okay and continued down the hallway.

About two weeks later he entered my office and asked if he could close the door.

"Sure, Spike. What's up?"

He looked down at the floor before continuing. "Well, Joe, the guys would really like you to join us at the academy football games. We all know how hard it is to get along on a technical sergeant's retirement pay so we 'passed the hat' and collected enough money to purchase season tickets for you and your wife."

I was so shocked that at first I didn't know what to say. "You passed the hat to raise money to buy me a season ticket because you think I can't afford it on my retired technical sergeant's pay? How embarrassing," I replied once I'd found my voice.

"First of all, I am not a retired tech sergeant." I reached into my pocket and pulled out my wallet, then opened it and removed my military ID card, which I handed to him. "Spike, I am a retired lieutenant colonel."

His jaw dropped and his face turned red as he returned the card to me. "What? I didn't know."

"I realize that," I replied. "But my question is why did you and the others think that I was a retired NCO?"

Spike appeared dumbfounded. "I don't know," he finally sputtered, "other than we just thought that you were."

I said, "I do not want to go because for five years I worked every Air Force Academy home football game in my dress blues. And those were long twelve-to-fourteen-hour days. The cadets had early morning parades in the cadet area before each game, which the security police had to monitor. Then we would reconfigure the troops for football traffic and crowd control. Of course we did not go home until the last fan had departed the academy. And I promised myself, 'My God, if I do not have to attend another Air Force Academy football game, I won't for a long time.' So that is why I don't want to attend. Believe me, it has nothing to do with money and not being able to afford the tickets."

"Joe, I know now and I am sorry," Spike stammered.

"Spike, don't be sorry," I offered. "Being prior service, I consider it an honor to be called a retired NCO."

Looking back I guess this episode showed that I did not wear my retired rank on my shoulders. However, it was obvious to me why Spike and the others thought I was a retired NCO: I was black. I had the trappings of a senior person at ARINC. I had my own private office, with two employees working for me, and I managed the security program, yet they assumed that I had to be an NCO. They never considered that I might be equal to or even senior to them in rank. The irony was, like most defense contractors, the majority of ARINC's employees were retired officers. As I recall, there was only one retired colonel, so as a retired lieutenant colonel, I was, in terms of military rank, equal to or senior to ninety-nine percent of my co-workers.

Was Spike a racist? I don't think so; I think he was just being honest in expressing his thoughts. Spike was not from the South; he had been raised on a farm in Ohio, graduated with an engineering degree from Ohio State University and spent more than twenty years in the Air Force. I still consider him one of my closest friends. We both live in the Colorado Springs area and for a while Ruby and I played in his church's bridge group. Like me, he is also a substitute teacher and we meet occasionally and discuss old times. But I still haven't forgotten the time he and our co-workers assumed I couldn't afford tickets to the academy football games.

ARINC had more than one thousand classified documents that needed to be assigned control numbers and entered into their system. Procedures needed to be written for checking documents in and out and many other administrative procedures had to be defined ASAP. The position also required a top-secret security clearance, which I had. I also operated their Sensitive Compartmented Information Facility (SCIF).

Hal Townend and I worked many long hours together and we met our self-imposed deadlines for getting everything done. When Hal returned to the San Diego office, I was charged with managing security in the office in Colorado Springs. Hal and I became very close. He had grown up in Washington, D.C., and was very proud of his Scottish ancestry. After a number of years of working together, I decided to ask Hal the question that had been bothering me for some time.

"Hal, why did you hire me for this job over the white applicants?"

He replied with a smile, "That's easy. You were the most qualified for the position."

"I figured as much," I said, "but employers don't always use that criterion for hiring people."

"Maybe not, but I certainly do."

That conversation must have had an impact on Hal because he flew in from San Diego to speak at my retirement luncheon in February 2000 and during his speech he made reference to that conversation. He said that he had chosen me over four other qualified applicants and that I had made him proud of that selection, a selection he never once regretted.

Even though I found success working in the civilian world in the years following my retirement from the Air Force, I found it hard, if not impossible, to go to the Air Force Academy again due to the lack of support I received from the academy itself. Although I lived, and in fact still live, only about six miles from the academy's main gate, I never went there except for medical emergencies or doctor visits. If my family and I wanted to use the commissary and base exchange, we would either drive the approximately twenty miles to Peterson Air Force Base or the thirty miles to Fort Carson.

The only reason I was able to go to the academy at all during emergencies was because of the support I received from retired NCOs and in some situations there, Bobby Harlan, Prep School, Bobby King,

Transportation Sq., Norris and Diane Williams, Social Actions, Albert and Vivian Holland, Social Actions, Gary Denham, Logistic Squadron, Richard Dubois, Air Academy Bank, Herman Johnson and Jose Fernandez, Airmen's Dining Hall, all of whom lived in the Colorado Springs area. We would run into each other at stores or on the street and invariably the conversation would turn to why I had retired so early. They convinced me that it wasn't anything that I had done that caused the vendetta against me, and that always lifted my spirits a great deal.

As I dealt with the end of my military career and my transition into civilian life, my wife, Ruby, was busy building her own career. She spent eleven years working as a therapist for the community mental health center for El Paso, Teller and Park Counties in Colorado. During that time she became very dissatisfied with the lack of individualized treatment given to the mentally ill, and the stigma attached to the clients who had no other choice for treatment. So in March 1990, Ruby and I founded Hoffler & Associates Counseling Service, Inc. At the time of its founding, Hoffler & Associates was the only African-American female-owned counseling agency in El Paso County, Colorado.

The founding philosophy of Hoffler & Associates was the acknowledgment that the mentally ill are unique people with different needs. Their potential skills, limitations and strengths must be addressed in their individualized treatment planning, goals and objectives. Over time, our mission at Hoffler & Associates evolved. Originally we focused on clients who were eligible for entitlements because of their severe and persistent mental illness. Eventually we expanded our mission to developing programs designed to address the needs of ethnic minorities, women and people with substance-abuse issues.

Hoffler & Associates Counseling Service, Inc. was initially capitalized by nothing more than our savings and credit cards. For many years, Ruby did not receive a salary and to this day I still do not draw a salary from the business even as we have funded the company since its founding. During the initial years, Ruby and I provided loans to meet payroll and take care of the bills.

In March 1990, Hoffler & Associates consisted of two Medicaid clients, a desk, two chairs, and a commitment by Ruby to provide individualized treatment to low-income mentally ill people in attractive surroundings. By 2005, Hoffler & Associates Counseling was still serving the citizens of El Paso County with the majority of its clients billed via insurance and a sliding fee scale. Ruby also remained busy as a member of the Board of Directors at Beth Heaven Group Home, along with retired Generals Ben Ellis and Ken Curtis.

Wanting to expand my commitment to the community, I began teaching fathering classes and volunteering my time at the Center on Fathering, providing services for young men who are struggling in their roles as fathers.

After retiring from ARINC, I also became a certified mediator and began volunteering as a mediator for the El Paso County district attorney's office, Neighborhood Justice Center, and the El Paso County Small Claims Court.

As much as I tried to get on with my life in the civilian world, there were always things that brought me right back to what had happened in 1984. In the back of my mind I always knew that I would return to my quest for justice one day, when the time was right.

This same situation would happen years later, in 2003, when the sexual abuse scandal surfaced at the academy. In that case, the female cadets who made complaints against the USAF Academy to their congressional representatives found that the Air Force turned around and investigated the complainants rather than try to address their concerns.

One of the most shocking developments during my post-retirement years, and one of the key events that re-awakened my desire for justice, was the sexual assault scandal that rocked the Air Force Academy in 2003. As shocking as the claims were, even more shocking were the allegations that when these women came forward with their allegations, their commanders made sure that they were punished, ignored, ostracized, or even subjected to further abuse in retaliation for reporting the incidents. It was obvious to me that the academy's methods of handling complaints had not changed much in eighteen years. Their policy was still to punish the person who filed the complaint rather than deal with the allegations. In addition, many of the sexual assault victims felt that they had not been supported by their commanders or by the academy staff when they came forward with their complaints.

The similarities between my case and the cases of these female cadets were striking. I grieved for what those young female cadets endured, and it made me furious to think that perhaps if my case had been handled properly, the atmosphere and culture at the academy might have improved enough by early 2000 that these abuses would not have taken place. At least I was impressed that someone had finally shown the fortitude to investigate the Air Force Academy beyond the perfunctory "face-saving" investigations of the past. It was my own senator from Colorado who spearheaded the investigation into the sexual assaults. The senator clearly had the attention of the secretary of the Air Force and the Air Force chief of staff. I began to feel hopeful again. I told Ruby, "After eighteen years maybe it's time for me to contact my senator and bring my case back out into the open."

Ruby supported me 100 percent, even though she worried about the effects of stress on my health following the open-heart bypass surgery I had in 1998.

I met with a member of the senator's staff, and informed her of the racism, the tampering with performance reports, the intimidation of witnesses, and the lying by senior officials at the academy that I had experienced in 1984. We both agreed that if anyone could assist me, it would be the senator because he had the attention of the Air Force. She recommended that I put my information in writing for him. So I went to the infamous Xerox box in my closet, read though the material and put together a presentation.

Meanwhile, in December 2000, I had begun working as a substitute teacher in Colorado Springs. One day in 2003 as I was working as a substitute, I was checking in with the school secretary when a heavy-set Asian man passed by and caught my eye.

"No, it can't be. Who is that?" I asked the secretary.

"Mr. Sung," she replied.

"I can't believe it. What a small world."

I had not seen the man in more than eighteen years, and even then I had only seen him for a few hours, but his image remained in my memory. Incredibly, with only a brief passing glance, I instantly remembered him.

"What's his room number?" I asked.

She gave me his room number and I went to see him. I felt rather nervous as I entered.

For eighteen years I had longed for the opportunity to ask him, "Given the hard evidence you had about the chief of staff's actions against me, why did you write up your report the way you did?" But I never thought that I would see the HQ USAF investigating officer again. And here we were working in the same building.

"Colonel, are you retired Air Force?" I asked, entering his classroom.

"Yes, I am. But you can call me Jeff."

"I'm Lieutenant Colonel Joseph Hoffler, retired," I began. "I was the Security Police Squadron commander at the Air Force Academy. You conducted a congressional investigation on me and my squadron."

He looked puzzled. "I don't remember doing a congressional investigation on you."

Sensing that he did not want to discuss the issue any further, I did not press him although my curiosity was piqued.

"Joe, come over here and see the pictures of my grandkids," he offered.

As we talked he explained that after he retired from the military, he went back to school and got his teaching certificate. Then students began entering the classroom, so I excused myself and left.

I could not wait to get home that night to tell Ruby who I had run into at school. She could not believe it either. The HQ USAF investigating officer, the person I had been hoping to meet someday, was right there at a school where I'd been subbing. He even lived in Colorado Springs.

Then I called the captain and relayed the story to him. He said, "Colonel H., I'm pumped. It is not like you saw this guy in a store or someplace; now you know where he is every day."

"But, Captain, he says he doesn't remember doing the congressional inquiry on me."

"Colonel H., that is bull. He couldn't have forgotten."

"I am telling you, he said he did not conduct a congressional investigation at the academy."

"Is it possible you got the wrong guy?"

"Not a chance. He's a retired Air Force colonel, previously stationed at Peterson AFB. It has been eighteen years and I recognized him right away."

"Colonel H., this guy really made an impression on you."

"Yes, he certainly did. If he had told the truth and submitted a true report after the inquiry, my whole life would be different today," I explained.

He concurred. "Yes, and the Air Force Academy would be different, too. Maybe there would not have been the cover-up of the sexual harassment cases either because the Air Force Academy would have corrected their procedures based on the HQ USAF investigating officer's report. That is some heavy stuff."

"Captain, it was like he really did not want to talk about it," I added. "Instead he directed me to pictures of his grandkids, stories about his kids, things like that."

"Colonel H., his reactions prove that the Air Force got to him. I told you that when I spoke to him all those years ago, he appeared to be very upset about what had happened to you."

"That's right."

As I recall, on the first day of the inquiry, he had seemed okay with investigating my claims. I could tell from the expressions on his face that he found the information I was giving him to be beyond belief, such as the illegal upgrading of Stover's APR, cleansing of his personnel file, transfer to another Air Force base, and the intimidation of witnesses. The second time he called me in, it was with a whole different set of questions. At that point it was more about investigating me than about the chief of staff's actions.

For example, the investigation report revealed that he became more concerned about finding "deep throat" within the academy personnel section, who leaked the information that A1C Stover's APR was illegally removed from his records, upgraded, rewritten and signed by the chief of staff, than he was about the seriousness of the actions. He even blamed a sergeant who worked in the airmen's report section, whose spouse worked in the Security Police Squadron, of leaking the information. The academy's chief of staff and the inspector general were racist, but they weren't too smart.

Actually, no one leaked the information. The personnel system worked the way it was designed to work. Even though the chief of staff and the inspector general had physically transferred A1C Stover to the Civil Engineer Squadron, as there wasn't a slot for a security policeman there, on paper he was still assigned to the Security Police Squadron. So when his APR was changed, the computer sent a printout to his squadron of record, the Security Police Squadron. The HQ USAF investigating officer seemed peeved when I showed him the printout. He asked very firmly how I got that information. I told him that I was A1C Stover's squadron commander and was authorized to have that printout. That was the "smoking gun" that showed the chief of staff and the inspector general had violated Air Force regulations. I guess we'll never know for sure what happened, but I feel as if the Air Force IG got to him and made him change his approach to ensure that the Air Force Academy was never found guilty of anything.

I continued to see the HQ USAF investigating officer when I substituted at that school and he was always very friendly to me. "Hi, Joe, how's it going? How was your class?" he would ask as we passed in the halls. Frankly, his friendly demeanor surprised me, given everything that had happened. I wondered how, in the summary of his congressional report, he could have overlooked the sworn statements from at least three white members of the squadron who told him that there was concern that "Blacks were running the squadron." Those comments in his report confirmed what the day shift flight chief, the security police investigator and my secretary had told me earlier, that the actions against me were racially motivated. So how could the HQ USAF investigating officer and the rest of the Air Force ignore those clearly racist remarks? Why didn't he investigate further and get to the bottom of those comments?

Those events took place in 1984, not in 1884. A black person should have been able to command a squadron at the United States Air Force Academy without being subjected to trumped-up charges and removed from his command simply because some whites could not accept the reality of having a black commander.

CHAPTER 17

FAILED ATTEMPTS FOR CONGRESSIONAL ASSISTANCE

Following the advice from the senator's staff member, I submitted my first letter to the senator early in 2003, asking him to reopen my case. I highlighted the fact that the time was right to reopen it based on the recent sexual assault scandal and the new willingness by the Air Force to explore practices and attitudes at the academy. I made it clear that I wasn't equating what had happened to me with what had happened to the female cadets who had been assaulted; I was simply making a point about changing attitudes and what appeared to be a new, more open policy at the USAF Academy.

In my long and detailed letter, I shared a bit about my background and the circumstances that led to me being denied a promotion. I made a clear delineation of what the chief of staff had done and how he and his co-conspirators had been able to run their conspiracy unchecked by the Air Force hierarchy. I described how the chief of staff violated Air Force regulations, intimidated witnesses, and abused his authority, all in his quest to deny me my well-deserved promotion.

I went on to describe my early career and the numerous career milestones I had reached. I also related my tours of duty in Thailand and England, my assignment to the academy and my five years of outstanding service there. I attached copies of my service records and went on to detail the chief of staff's refusal to grant my request for an extension, A1C Stover's actions and the chief of staff's investigation, the undeserved letter of reprimand, and everything that happened afterwards. I included lots of documentation to show my longstanding quest for justice against these trumped-up charges. My letter concluded:

> *Senator Allard, the true evaluation of my performance as security police commander at the Air Force Academy can be taken from the other ninety-nine percent of my troops and 100 percent of my supervisors prior to working for the chief of staff for only ten days. My performance reports are attached and there is evidence throughout the report that my operations officer and first sergeant stayed with me throughout the character assassination campaign by the chief of staff. They worked very closely with me daily. They knew better.*
>
> *However, my goal is to right a wrong that has persisted for more than nineteen years. My goal is not publicity or revenge against the chief of staff. The chief of staff has to live with himself. He knows what he did to me was based on my race and was wrong. I feel that for the first time in more than nineteen years, someone with authority is questioning the Air Force Academy and how the Air Force investigates complaints against the Air Force Academy.*
>
> *Sincerely,*
> *Lt. Col. Retired Joseph W. Hoffler, USAF*

I felt satisfied that my letter made a strong and consistent argument as to why now was the time for the senator to reopen my case. I sent it with the hope and expectation that at last I would be listened to and would receive an appropriate response. Instead of the response I had hoped for I received a letter, dated March 21, 2003, from the department of the Air Force, office of the inspector general, written and signed by a major, chief of the high-level inquiries branch. The letter read:

Dear Lieutenant Colonel Hoffler:

Senator Wayne Allard's office forwarded to the Air Force inspector general's Inquiries Directorate your 3 March 2003 complaint regarding your experience at the United States Air Force Academy dating to 1984 and earlier. Thank you for taking the time to organize and present an excellently framed allegation. However, the amount of time elapsed since the events you describe seriously impedes an IG's ability to gather sufficient evidence and testimony to determine the facts concerning your allegation. For this reason, an IG investigation into your complaint will not be conducted.

I know this is not the answer you were looking for but please be assured that we reviewed your complaint thoroughly before reaching this determination. I am forwarding a copy of this correspondence to the Air Force Legislative Liaison Office, which will notify Senator Allard's office in Colorado Springs of your complaint disposition.

Thank you for bringing this matter to our attention.

My first response upon receiving this letter was, "I did not know that there was a statue of limitation on racism in the military."

I consulted with Ruby and the captain. "What should I do now?" I asked. Their response was simple: I needed to send a follow-up letter to Senator Allard, which is what I did at the end of March 2003.

In this second letter I didn't mince any words. I wrote:

I applaud your actions, Senator John Warner (R-VA), and other members of Congress who have brought about changes at the Air Force Academy. It is sad to state, however, that it has been proven that the Air Force cannot investigate incidents at the Air Force Academy. There was a mentality there that the reputation of the USAF Academy was more important than the individual. Under such a mentality, women and racial minorities served at the mercy of their supervisors and commanders. If his or her supervisor was unethical and treated them in a discriminatory fashion, not only did the Air Force fail to conduct an impartial investigation and correct the situation, as we see with the women cadets, the person who filed a complaint was usually punished.

I went on to describe once again how every Air Force agency neglected to properly investigate my case and failed to address the underlying racism that had ended my military career.

Senator Allard, by no means am I attempting to equate sexual assault with racial discrimination. However, now that the Air Force Academy is finally answering to members of Congress, I feel that it is also important that members of Congress do not forget the active duty Air Force members who served honorably on the Air Force Academy and who were victims of racial discrimination. Justice should be sought for those Air Force members also. I sincerely hope that there is not a 'statue of limitation' for racial discrimination in the military. Justice for me will be meeting a promotion board and being selected for promotion to colonel.

I ended my letter with the admonishment:

Now that you have the Air Force's attention, I expect the Air Force to give you the respect that it did not give Senator Armstrong in 1984.

When this letter also failed to elicit any sort of reply, I wrote the senator once again at the beginning of April 2003. This time I enclosed a copy of the letter I had received from a major informing me that it was too late to open a new investigation into my case. I knew I had to take an increasingly tough tone with the senator if I hoped to get any kind of response. I wrote:

The attached letter from SAF/IGQ is surprising. After you and other

*members of Congress successfully peeled back the cover of invincibility
from the Air Force Academy, one would think that the Air Force would
be more amenable to conducting investigations into incidents at the Air
Force Academy... However, I was wrong. The Air Force is going to dig
its heels in until it is dragged into the 21st century by members of
Congress.*

I described yet again what had happened to me and explained how the senator and others could begin their investigation into the wrongdoings
perpetrated against me and other black officers at the academy in 1984.

*I offered the Air Force the opportunity to settle my complaint quietly.
I don't want to make a media civil rights issue out of this. However, it
doesn't take much for citizens to ask the Air Force, 'How are you dealing with issues of racial discrimination at the Air Force Academy?'
I guess it is rather obvious now that the Air Force still considers itself
outside of the power of Congress.*

I closed my letter with...

*Senator Allard, I sincerely hope that the reply from SAF/IGQ is not your
final reply. Now that the country is aware that the Air Force cannot be
trusted to investigate sensitive allegations at the Air Force Academy, my
allegation has more credibility.*

Refusing to believe that was his final reply and wanting to give Senator
Allard one more chance, I sent him yet another personal letter on
February 27, 2004. I began by reminding him:

*The previous March I had submitted to you a well-documented case of
a 'high-tech lynching' (to borrow a phrase from a noted Republican,
Supreme Court Justice Clarence Thomas) by the officials at the Air
Force Academy. The then-chief of staff, the chief of staff and academy*

inspector general collaborated to ensure that I wasn't promoted to the rank of colonel. I submitted to you documented evidence that their actions were racially motivated and violated Air Force regulations. The details were outlined in my submission. All I received back was the typical 'stone-walling' letter from SAF/IG stating that nineteen years was too long to investigate my case.

Naturally, I was shocked to read an article in the Colorado Springs Gazette, dated February 22, 2004, titled 'Air Force medal awarded 40 years late,' and subtitled, 'Allard's staff secured lost commendation for retired major.' The obvious question from me is, why didn't I receive the same level of assistance? If the Air Force can research back sixty years across many countries in the Pacific, one would think that it could research back nineteen years on one installation. Why can your staff cut through the bureaucracy for Major Richard Lange and not for Lt. Col. Hoffler? As a citizen of the state of Colorado, I feel that is a fair question.

Senator Allard, as a member of the Senate Armed Services Committee, I am sure you are aware the Air Force is not going to act on this matter unless pressed to act. Therefore, I respectfully request that you readdress my case to the Air Force.

Senator Allard, although I am not looking for publicity, I would love to take a picture shaking your hand for the local newspapers while my wife of thirty-nine years pins on my colonel's insignia, which was wrongly denied twenty years ago.

Yet again I received no response from Senator Allard and finally had to accept that for whatever reason, he was not willing to reopen my case and help alleviate more than twenty years of gross injustice.

EPILOGUE

As I write this book in 2008, I have no regrets over joining the Air Force in 1962, even considering everything that has happened since then. Back then, the Air Force offered me the opportunity to "compete on a level playing field" and I relished that opportunity. The civilian community in 1962, particularly in the South, certainly could not have offered me the same opportunities for equality and advancement. So many significant events in the Civil Rights Movement happened after I enlisted in the Air Force. I felt like an eyewitness to history as I watched the March on Washington in 1963, President Lyndon Johnson signing the Civil Rights Bill in 1965 and the passage of the Voting Rights Act that same year.

The majority of my college classmates went into the teaching profession because that was one of the few professions open to blacks during that time. Of course nearly all of the city, state, and county jobs across the country were taken by whites. So the only way to get an equal opportunity in employment for a black person was to acquire a federal position, which was why I chose to enlist in the Air Force.

From September 1962, when I enlisted in the Air Force, until March 11, 1984, when a new chief of staff became my supervisor, a period of almost twenty-two years, I can honestly state that I competed and excelled at every turn. It is true that during those two decades I sometimes encountered racial insensitivities, but when those incidents were brought to the attention of senior supervisors and commanders, they were quickly corrected.

Perhaps that is why I was so shocked when I first realized the Air Force Academy's "in-your-face" institutional racism. Nothing in my career leading up to that point suggested that could happen. For reasons unknown to me, the chief of staff was able to operate without retribution or fear of being held accountable for his racist actions. It was as if he held power and authority outside of the Air Force over senior members at the Air Force Academy and no one dared to challenge him.

One thing that is certain is that the superintendent and the chief of staff of the USAF Academy operated their own personal system of rewards and punishments. The people who supported the chief of staff's racist plans, either through their actions or through their silence, were rewarded. In the process of writing this book I realized that it was important for me to spell out exactly how these rewards and punishments were meted out, person by person, for those involved in my case. For example:

The superintendent: He revoked my Meritorious Service medal after I retired from the Air Force as revenge for my contacting my senator from Colorado. However, armed with sworn statements given to the congressional investigator from the NCOIC and the airman who worked in personnel that A1C Stover's APR was illegally removed and replaced with one signed by the chief of staff, the superintendent gave the chief of staff a full military retirement with honors and medals.

Airman Brett Stover: He lied under testimony and provided the "dirt" for the inspector general investigation against me. His reward was to have his performance report illegally upgraded, his personnel record was illegally cleansed, and he was illegally restored to duty as a fully qualified security policeman and illegally transferred to another Air

Force base, a transfer that the Air Force, and therefore the taxpayers, paid for. His transfer was necessary to stop him from bragging around the squadron that he was on a special assignment for the inspector general and chief of staff.

Even with all of those favorable actions, Stover was still discharged from the USAF within a year by his new commander. The assessment of A1C Stover's fitness for military life by me, the captain and the first sergeant was vehemently criticized by the chief of staff, the inspector general and the HQ USAF Academy's investigating officer. However, our assessment of Stover for the military was verified on at least three occasions. His new commander agreed with us that A1C Stover was not fit for military life and discharged him within a year of arriving in his squadron; the recruiter for a large police department in Texas stated that there was no way he would issue A1C Stover a weapon; and Col. Sung, the HQ USAF investigating officer, tried his best to get my successor to criticize my decision to withdraw A1C Stover's weapon. However, as a Security Police Squadron commander, he stated, given the information I had about A1C Stover's personal problems, he would have taken the same actions. The decision to withdraw a person's weapon is not taken lightly because that is one less person you have to work the posting.

The USAF Academy's investigating officer lied in his report and threatened and cussed at witnesses who did not give him the answers he wanted. He only interviewed witnesses who had been referred to him by A1C Stover and failed to notify me that he was performing an official inspector general investigation. In addition he failed to inform me that I was a suspect in the theft of government property and denied me access to the investigation report, both of which were required by Air Force regulations.

The USAF Academy's investigating officer's reward for his actions was promotion to the academy's inspector general position the following month. In addition he was promoted to colonel on the next promotion board, the promotion board at which I should have been promoted to colonel.

The academy's social actions officer, after receiving my complaint, briefed the chief of staff on my complaint and allowed him to choose his personal friend to do the investigation on him. He refused to do the investigation on the chief of staff himself, even though it was his responsibility. His reward for his actions was a promotion to lieutenant colonel on the next promotion board.

The chief of CBPO, the Central Base Personnel Office: He was the officer in charge of the personnel records section at the academy. He was made aware of the chief of staff's approved raid on, and the illegal documentation of, the personnel records of Airman Brett Stover. He did not stop these illegal actions, nor did he report them to the proper authorities, as he was required to do. His reward was promotion to lieutenant colonel on the next promotion board.

The chief master sergeant of the Security Police Squadron: He supplied false information to the chief of staff at his request and expressed concern about too many blacks being in leadership positions in the Security Police Squadron. Because he was already on the highest enlisted rank, he could not be promoted but he did get his wishes of seeing senior blacks removed from their positions of authority and having a black commander replaced with a white one. In addition he had the honor of having the academy superintendent, a three-star general, attend his retirement ceremony, the same general who refused to attend mine.

The captain called and asked me to attend the chief's retirement ceremony. Initially I said that I did not want to go to another security police function. However, the captain, being as insistent as always, kept asking me to come. He said that some of the troops wanted to see me again. Not wanting to disappoint the troops, I reluctantly agreed to attend. I expected to see the chief of staff there, which he was. However, I did not expect to see the superintendent. He had refused to attend my retirement ceremony from the Air Force. However, he attended the retirement ceremony for the chief, the person who led the "racial mutiny" of whites against the blacks in leadership positions in the 7625th Security Police Squadron. By attending the retirement ceremony for the chief, his position (superintendent of the USAF Academy) and his rank (three-star general) gave instant credibility to their cause. To those there who attended both retirement ceremonies, mine and the chief's, the superintendent's attendance spoke loudly: "I endorse the actions by the chief of staff and the chief to make a change in the racial makeup of the squadron's command element."

Lt. Cols. Slade and Louis: These two were black instructors at the academy. In February 1984, Lt. Col. Slade expressed concerns about the lack of racial diversity at the academy and the fact that he had been passed over for a permanent professor's position in favor of a white instructor. To address those concerns he called a meeting of the five most senior black officers assigned to the academy. In that meeting both black professors were very militant about the lack of black officers and senior NCOs at the academy. They suggested we schedule a meeting with the superintendent to discuss remedies. Both mentioned that I was the only black officer out of four left in the chief of staff's area. I said that since the present colonel had become the chief of personnel, no additional black officers had been assigned to the chief of staff's area. The meeting ended with a commitment from all attendees to bring more black officers and senior NCOs to the Air Force Academy.

When I mentioned this meeting in my social action complaint, neither black professor was willing to support me. Lt. Col. Slade was given a quick and "choice" one-year assignment to the Pentagon with the assurance of a promotion to colonel and a position as commandant of the preparatory school once he returned to the academy. Meanwhile, Lt. Col. Louis' reward was a promotion from being an obscure instructor in the dean of faculty area to the prime position of the academy inspector general.

The actions of these black professors really hit a raw nerve with me. I had known both of them since I first arrived at the USAF Academy and I had considered both of them my friends. We socialized after duty hours, played golf together and considered ourselves proud members of the fraternity of Air Force officers who were graduates of HBCUs. (historically black colleges/universities). We were close to the same age and, therefore, our generation was on the forefront of the civil right battles in America. They both talked a good game about equal rights for all. However, when the time came to stand up against racial discrimination at the USAF Academy, they both sat down and sold out for their own personal gains.

I contrast the actions of Lt. Cols. Slade and Louis with those of the captain and first sergeant, whom I had known far less time than I knew Lt. Cols. Slade and Louis. Both the captain and first sergeant risked their Air Force careers in the fight against racial discrimination, while the professors accepted their appeasement promotions and assignments and kept quiet. The first sergeant wrote a letter to the superintendent telling him about the situation and asking for his support. And the day shift flight chief, the security police investigator and my secretary, all black enlisted personnel, asked if there was anything they could do to assist in the battle against racial discrimination at the USAF Academy.

USAF captain, legal officer: He was my military attorney who did absolutely nothing for me beyond writing a letter to the chief of staff essentially begging him not to take disciplinary action against me. He did not see any of the evidence against me, nor did he interview any witnesses. In my opinion he was worse than having a public defender and in this case the Air Force failed to provide me with adequate legal representation. His reward for doing the very minimum on my case was a promotion to major. He didn't want to risk his promotion by going up against the Air Force Academy to support me.

As I consider the list of people who were rewarded for working against me, I must also list the people who suffered negative ramifications for speaking out or acting on my behalf. For example:

The captain: My operations officer was threatened by the chief of staff with a letter of reprimand and removal from his position if he continued to aid me in my case.

First sergeant: The first sergeant was threatened with being relieved of his position because he wrote a letter to the superintendent informing him that the investigation against me was nothing more than a witch hunt and that the academy was threatening squadron personnel and cussing at them. The chief of staff referred to him as "that stupid sergeant."

The NCOIC of operations: The chief of staff opened a closed case against him that was more than eight months old, found him guilty and directed that his commander give him a letter of reprimand.

The NCOIC of pass and ID: He made the mistake of thinking that the chief of staff wanted to hear the truth. He went to see the chief of staff but when he made positive statements on my behalf, the chief of staff yelled at him and told him to leave his office.

The NCOIC of supply: The USAF Academy's investigating officer tried to threaten and coerce him into giving information that would incriminate me with the theft of government property. The Security Police Squadron's supply NCOIC refused and instead would only tell the truth.

Looking over my list, I see that it is a sad indictment of what can happen when racism is left to fester unchecked. It wasn't just my career that was destroyed; many people paid the price for the faults of the corrupt system that allowed this to happen. That is why I am writing this book, so no other young member of the U.S. Armed Forces will suffer such a miscarriage of justice.

Living as I do in Colorado Springs, every year around graduation time at the academy the local newspaper publishes long, glowing articles and lavish photographs of the ceremony. Seeing that is always hard for me, remembering the graduation in 1984 when I was unfairly blamed for the cancellation of the Thunderbirds fly-over.

Graduation at the United States Air Force Academy is a culmination of two weeks of activities—parades, social events, etc.—that take place the last week of May. The Security Police Squadron is always tasked to the maximum, having to provide the day-to-day security in addition to providing personnel for "June Week" (even though they take place in May) events.

As I read the newspaper, I see warnings to the attendees to arrive early, to avoid the crowds, that tickets will be required to enter the stadium, that metal detectors will be used and that everyone will be searched. Such warnings were not given to the public for the graduation ceremony in May of 1984. I remember sitting in the command post with the NCOIC security police operations and NCOIC plans and programs, trying to find additional people to help move the crowd so that the Thunderbirds could fly. But there just were not enough people available. I was blamed by the chief of staff for the Thunderbirds being unable to fly that day, but one of my favorite mementos from my retirement is a picture of a Thunderbird fly-over of the academy, presented to me by the members of the Security Police Squadron on the day I retired.

It brought tears to my eyes when the "B" flight chief, who made the presentation, said, "Colonel, we know that you are being blamed for the Thunderbirds not flying during the academy graduation, and we feel very sorry for what happened. However, we want you to know that we appreciated everything you did that day and we know that you were not responsible. Please accept this as a token of our appreciation for your hard work and look at it every graduation day and remember us." With bittersweet memories I most definitely do think about that event every graduation day and consider all the graduation days I missed because of what was done to me in the name of racism.

The greater tragedy of my case, beyond what happened to me, was the disenfranchisement of the brave men and women of the 7625th Security Police Squadron. They witnessed a great miscarriage of military justice, which was obviously racially motivated.

Many risked their careers in a failed attempt to bring fairness to the process and to follow the "Security Police Creed," which reads in part: "I perform my duties in a firm, courteous, and impartial manner, irrespective of a person's color, race, religion or national origin."

Webster's Dictionary defines racism as "the practice of racial discrimination." I define it as "high-tech lynching" when a racist goes beyond discrimination and publicly and personally attacks a fellow human being in an attempt to belittle, degrade, humiliate, or remove that person's self-esteem. In other words, the things that were done to me constitute a high-tech lynching. Still the underlying factor remains

A photo of the Thunderbirds presented by TSgt. Boyd at my retirement.

that the Air Force cannot take from me what it did not give to me in the first place. Surely it can take away my uniform, ribbons and awards, but it cannot take away my pride in myself and in my race, my dignity, and my self-respect, all of which I received from my parents. I was a proud black man when I enlisted in the Air Force in 1962 and I remained the same proud black man when I left the Air Force twenty-two years later. I am that same proud black man today. Nothing the chief of staff could do could ever remove those characteristics from my DNA. This is who I will be until the day I die.

I was certainly aware of instances in which the other branches of the military—the Army, the Navy and the Marines—had taken action to correct past discrimination against African-Americans in the areas of promotion, awarding of medals, court-martials, disciplinary actions and discharges and other such things.

For example, the Navy has recently reviewed the cases of the African-American sailors involved in the Port of Chicago incident in 1944 and the Army has also recently reviewed the case of a black chaplain wrong-fully and dishonorably discharged in 1894, more than 100 years ago.

An article in *The Gazette,* July 2, 2005, details that the Army formally overturned the 1984 dishonorable discharge of its first black chaplain, Henry Vinton Plummer, who struggled for years to overturn the dishonorable discharge and court-martial. They said the discharge and court-martial were made on little evidence by an all-white judicial panel that convicted because of his race. If one fast-fowards ninety years, the first black squadron commander in the Air Force Academy is disciplined because of his race on little evidence based on an unprofessionally conducted investigation with evidence given by an all-white panel. Yet the Air Force wants us to believe that it can't investigate a well-documented case of discrimination from only twenty-one years ago?

An article in the *Denver Post* dated May 10, 2005, details efforts by U.S. Rep. Diana DeGette (D-CO) to obtain a promotion for a female African-American Army social worker who was denied promotion from private first-class during World War II based on her race and gender. Yet the Air Force is digging in its heels and denying that any discrimination has taken place in the Air Force since its formation in 1947?

When white service members have been wronged, the Air Force is willing to acknowledge and correct its earlier mistakes. For example, an article in *The Gazette* dated February 22, 2005, describes the efforts that my senator from Colorado and the Air Force made to ensure that a retired Air Force major and World War II veteran received his long-overdue medal.

My great hope in writing this story is that it will serve to make life better for the present and future minorities who are or will be assigned to the Air Force Academy. To verify institutionalized racial discrimination at the USAF Academy, one needs to look no further than the position of permanent professor, a position in which the professor receives tenure and is promoted to brigadier general upon retirement. Since its beginning, the USAF Academy has had only one black permanent professor and he retired in the 1980s, before being promoted to brigadier general. Since the 1980s, many black professors have applied and only one in 2008 has been chosen for permanent professor. Blacks are good enough to die on the battlefield but not good enough to be named to the much coveted position of permanent professor at the USAF Academy. General Colin Powell was once quoted as saying, "Don't walk around with the color of your skin on your shoulder waiting for someone to knock it off. That's their problem. If they look at you that way or they want to discriminate against you or they hold the wrong attitudes against you, that's their problem. And what you have to do is perform and defeat their stereotype. If you don't perform, then they'll hold that prejudice, but if you do perform and take advantage of all of the opportunities you have, then there's nothing they can do to stop you."

Far be it for me to contradict someone as honored and as decorated as General Powell; however, I must disagree with him here. In my case I did perform, I took advantage of all the opportunities that were presented to me and still they stopped me, and all because of the color of my skin. My passionate plea to all of my fellow Americans is please, do not let this happen ever again. Only then will my struggle not have been in vain.

The academy chief of staff (the "sheriff") and the inspector general ("police chief") operated like the top officials in a small town in which they had an "uppity" black man to put down. They executed their plan to "put me in my place" to perfection. How dare this black officer think he was going to get promoted to colonel during their era? As I was going to be found guilty of all charges anyway, all they needed was a white person to make a complaint against me, no matter how frivolous or how truthful. Then they hand picked their investigating officer ("district attorney") to ensure they got the verdict they wanted. Although there was concern about too many blacks being in senior positions in the squadron, the investigating officer, to get the desired answers, only questioned white security police personnel (the "jury").

The only black person who was allowed a voice was the superintendent's investigating officer and since his analysis of the facts did not fit the presumption of guilty, it was denied.

However, all of this operation rested on the shoulders of the superintendent of the Air Force Academy (the "mayor"). He did not want to know anything about what was going on. He stuck his head in the sand and refused to hear anything. When I requested to speak, he told me he did not want to hear anything I had to say.

I was not advised of the fact that I was being investigated, not read my Article 31 rights, not allowed to see the investigative report. Blacks don't get such rights under the above described scenario. However, in real life, that scenario did not take place in some small Southern town in the Jim Crow era. It took place on United States government property, the USAF Academy in the 1980s. And as an American citizen, my constitutional rights were violated.

My story is unique in that the chief of staff was able to corrupt the whole system: my commander, a lieutenant general, the academy's inspector general, Social Actions and Staff Judge Advocate offices, which were put into place to protect military personnel from discrimination and loss of legal rights. All of them were negligent in performing their duties as mandated by the Air Force. Hence the implication of my quote at the beginning of this story, "The only thing necessary for the triumph of evil is for good men to do nothing." I have documented that those actions did occur and that the Air Force was aware of those violations and did nothing. This book will definitely answer the following question: Can the U.S. Congress, civil right organizations, and the U.S. Air Force "handle the truth"?